FREESTANDING

Maurice Jamall

ABAX

Dedication

For Brita Haycraft and in memory of her husband, John Haycraft C.B.E. whose early influence encouraged me to enter this marvelous profession

Published by ABAX Ltd.,
Tokyo, Japan and Vancouver, Canada

Editorial Office ● Tel: 81-44-813-2909 / Fax: 81-44-813-2916
email ● whats@abax.co.jp
homepage ● http://www.abax.co.jp

Layout, Cover Design, and Illustrations by Design Office TERRA

ISBN 1-896942-02-4

Foreword

Freestanding is a resource book for teachers of English to young adults and adults who are speakers of other languages. The book consists of thirty six lessons which cover a variety of topics and themes. This ensures that a range of language may be introduced and developed and generates a high level of interest on the part of the learners. The lessons are designed to encourage students to take more control over the language they learn and the way in which they choose to learn it. The book itself is designed to be taught with a minimum of materials. Almost half the lessons can be completed by a teacher using a board marker or a piece of chalk alone.

The teaching approach employed in this book is something perhaps best described as *Language Pull*. This describes a situation where learners are *pulling* the language that they want or need from the teacher rather than a situation where the teacher attempts to coax students into learning a series of predetermined lexical items or structures (*Language Push*). The teacher serves first and foremost as a Language Source and Lesson Director rather than as a Director of Input and Imparter of Knowledge. Key features of *Freestanding* include:

◆ A task-based approach to classroom procedure.
◆ Student-centered speaking and listening activities.
◆ Student-generated activities.
◆ Student-oriented language needs.
◆ Minimum preparation and handouts.

How To Use This Book

The book consists of thirty six lessons which cover about seventy hours of classroom time. Most lessons should take between sixty and ninety minutes to complete. In addition, lessons are organized around high-frequency topics which can be conveniently incorporated into any course. While we expect the majority of lessons to be executed as written, you, the teacher, will best be able to judge the appropriacy of the target language and content, as no two groups of students are the same and different cultures react differently to ideas and concepts. To give you an example, I started my teaching career in Nepal, a beautiful, mysterious and land-locked country. I had prepared what I thought was a rather good lesson on opinions, suggestions, agreeing and disagreeing, the final stage of which had the students planning a dream beach resort. Unfortunately, none of the students had ever seen a beach and did not expect to ever be wealthy enough to afford a trip to one even in neighboring India. Needless to say, the lesson died a slow and painful death! The materials were fine, (in fact the same lesson went very well a couple of years later in Thailand) but they were not culturally appropriate to that particular group of students.

Similarly, with time required for each lesson, it is important to remember that different groups of students will respond differently. You may find that some classes will be completed within sixty minutes and that others may require longer than the anticipated maximum time of ninety minutes.

Lessons have been constructed as a series of lesson plans. We have done this for two reasons: for ease of reference in the classroom and to create an element of consistency throughout the book.

Guide to Headings and Terms Used In The Lesson Plans

1. Level

The range of level at which this lesson may be successfully attempted. It should be remembered however, that as the lessons are, for the most part, student-generated learning experiences, it is more than possible that they could be taught at different levels.

2. Aims

What it is expected the lesson will achieve: what skills ought to be practiced, vocabulary and/or structures addressed and so on. Possibly the most important category in the plan, we strongly recommend that you read this section carefully.

3. Getting Ready

The materials you will need to successfully teach the lesson. In reality, this usually means either one or two blank pieces of paper per student or nothing at all.

4. Procedure

The actual stages of the lesson are given here. Written as an easy-to-follow, step-by-step guide, we anticipate that you will have very few problems concerning how to actually teach the lesson.

5. Warmer

This serves two purposes: to get students thinking in English quickly at the start of the class and to introduce the topic and language to be dealt with during the lesson. The warmers are generally easy and quite light affairs. As a rule of thumb, you can expect to spend about ten minutes on this part of the lesson.

6. Speaking/Writing/Listening/Reading

The main skill area that the students will be practising through execution of the task.

7. Variation

Suggests alternative activities or routes to achieve the specified aims. Warning: The variations usually require preparation of some kind: obtaining flashcards, cutting up pieces of paper and so on.

8. Language Focus

Some lessons have explicit linguistic aims. When this is so, this step in the procedure gives ideas regarding how to teach or review a specific area of the language system. Here, it is suggested that you focus more on accuracy than on fluency.

9. Drill Students

When you are introducing new vocabulary, have the students practise saying the word. You can do this with the whole class (chorally) having them repeat the word after you, or with just one or two students (individually) correcting them so that the other students can listen out for the correct form. As a rule of thumb, it's probably best to use a combination of the two: individually drill a couple of students and then chorally drill the whole class with each new word.

10. Monitor/Assist As Required

This cue suggests that you walk around the groups listening to what is being said. You can then use what you hear as a guide to future language input sessions. Students may turn to you and ask for specific vocabulary items or structures. Feel free to feed them in as required. If you choose to do any correction we recommend that you do so informally using techniques such as caretaker talk (echoing back the correct form when students make an error) rather than more explicit correction, as doing the latter will probably interfere with the task that the students are performing.

11. Feedback

The purpose of this is to round off a task with some meaning-based rather than language-based feedback. This is mainly to validate the task that the students have performed. That is, if you ask them to do something and then have no interest in the results, it will probably be demotivating for the students.

12. Teacher-Centered Listening

Some of the lessons require you to be the source of the listening material. There are several advantages to this. You can control the level of difficulty of the listening text and, as the topic is generally something personal about or to you, the students will be more interested in listening. Another advantage to using the teacher as a listening source is that it is *active listening*. Since the students are listening live, they will be able to react in real time to what they hear; asking you follow-up or clarification questions. This is what occurs in real world use of language and something that a pre-recorded listening text cannot achieve. Finally, an important part of the listening is the modeling of the student task to come. By first giving them the example, students will have a clearer idea about what to do when it comes to their turn to speak.

Following the guidelines outlined above should ensure a successful lesson. We hope you and your students find the ideas contained in *Freestanding* to be beneficial and we welcome any feedback you may care to send.

contents

1. Airports And Immigration

Aims
i.   To review/develop vocabulary related to airports.
ii. To give practice in the *going to* future.
iii. To give speaking practice in the context of an airport roleplay.

Getting Ready
Each student will need a piece of paper.

Procedure

Warmer

i.   Write two lists on the board:

Narita	Amsterdam
Orly	Tokyo
Schiphol	Paris
Changi	Washington
Dulles	Singapore

ii. In pairs, students match airport to its city. Add as many more as you wish.

Speaking: Airport Experiences

i.   Put the following on board:

How many airports have you been to?

Which is the nicest/worst? Why?

Which has the best duty-free service?

Do you like to get to the airport very early or not? Why?

How do you usually get to the airport?

ii. In pairs/small groups, students ask and answer the above questions.
iii. Monitor/assist as required. Join in if you want.

Vocabulary I: At The Airport

i.   Put the following categories on the board:

PEOPLE; PLACES; THINGS TO DO

ii. In pairs, students try to come up with as many items for each category as they can think of.
iii. Elicit one or two examples first so they get the idea.
iv. Monitor/assist as required.
v.   Feedback: Have one or two students come up to the board and write their ideas. Work on group spelling correction. Some pronunciation work could be done at this point.

Vocabulary II: Recycling And Reinforcing

i. In pairs, students put the items from *Vocabulary I* in the order in which they are done or encountered at the airport, from arriving there to getting on the plane.

Language Focus: "Going To…" In Questions

i. Ask students where they go to first when they arrive in a foreign country.
ii. Elicit: Immigration.
iii. Ask students what happens there.
iv. Elicit one or two questions that an immigration officer might ask a foreigner.
     e.g. "Can I see your passport?", "How long are you going to stay?" etc. …
v. In pairs, students then continue. Tell them to come up with at least eight questions for the immigration officer to ask.
vi. Monitor/assist as required. Check students use of target language.
vii. Feedback. Have some of the students come up to the board and write one question each.
viii. In pairs, students search for any errors in the questions (spelling, grammar etc. …).
ix. Correct students' work.

Roleplay: At The Immigration Counter

i. Tell students that they are going on holiday to America, Britain, or Canada (or any country you feel they may have knowledge of).
ii. Have them look at their list of questions again and give them a few minutes to think of possible answers.
iii. Give them a piece of blank paper (see: *Getting Ready*) on which to make any notes.
iv. Have students stand in two rows, like this:

	1	2	3	4	5	6	7
Students A x	x	x	x	x	x	x
Students B x	x	x	x	x	x	x

(Students A are immigration officers and Students B are travelers.)

v. Students roleplay the situation with the person opposite.
vi. When they have finished, student A7 comes to the end of the line and everyone moves up one position. Now students have new partners.
vii. Students roleplay the situation again to improve fluency.
viii. Student A6 then comes to the end of the line and everyone moves up one again.
ix. Students A are now travelers, students B are immigration officers. Roleplay situation as before.
x. Monitor and assist as required but less so on the second occasion as students should be able to do the roleplay on their own by now.
xi. Feedback: Get one of the better pairs to act out the situation for the rest of the class.

2. From Cradle To Grave

Aims
i. To give practice in the past simple tense.
ii. To teach verbs describing life's events: (born, marry, retire)
iii. To give students practice in speaking in the context of asking and answering questions about their lives.

Getting Ready
Students will need one piece of paper each. You will also need some adhesive tape or blue tack (see: *Warmer Variation* and *Speaking*)

Procedure

Warmer

Play *Twenty Questions*:

i. Put students into groups of four.
ii. One student thinks of a famous **dead** person.
iii. The other students have to find out his/her identity.
iv. The student being asked can only respond "yes," "no," "I don't know," or "it doesn't matter."
v. The three students have a limited number of questions with which to guess the mystery person. (Ten questions is usually sufficient).
vi. When the person is guessed, a second student thinks of a person and so on round the group.

Variation

i. Prepare slips of paper onto which you write the names of famous dead people.
ii. Stick a slip onto each student's back.
iii. Students mingle and ask questions in order to find out who they are supposed to be.

Vocabulary: Life's Events

i. Brainstorm things that people do in Life.
   NB: Be careful here. Students often come up with things like *eat*, *sleep* and so on. Stress that you want events rather than every day actions.
ii. Elicit one or two things, e.g. get married, die.
iii. Students then continue in pairs. Set a number of items you want from them (say 10).
iv. Monitor/assist as required.
v. Feedback: Put some ideas on the board.

Variation

For weaker groups, or if they just can't get the idea, put up a list on the board (born, get engaged, move house, leave home). Students put the events into some sort of logical order.

Language Focus: The Simple Past Tense

i. Write up on the board the life story of a famous person with the verbs in the base form.

ii. Students have to read it and guess who the person is.

iii. Students then reread and put the verbs in the correct form of the past tense.

iv. Make up your own or use the one provided below.

Model Life History

He (born) in Bromley, London in January, 1947. While he (be) still a schoolboy he (have) a fight with another boy over a girl. He (be) punched in the eye which (make) one of his eyes a different color. He (become) very famous for this later on in his life. After school he (go) to art college but (not/like) it very much. He (do) some acting and singing but he (not/be) very successful. He (meet) his future wife in the late sixties and they (get) married on March 20th 1970. His first big record (be) called *Space Oddity* which (come) out in 1969. It (reach) Number 5 in the UK charts. His records then (sell) well especially his third album, *Ziggy Stardust*. In the middle seventies he (move) to America and (start) taking lots of drugs, especially cocaine. Later he (settle) in Berlin where he (make) three records with Brian Eno. He (get) divorced in the early eighties but (remarry) in 1995. His new wife (be) the supermodel, Iman. He (make) several films in the seventies and eighties including *The Man who Fell to Earth*, *The Hunger*, *Just a Gigolo* and *The Last Temptation of Christ*. Today he (live) with his wife in Australia.

(Answer: David Bowie)

Language Work: Question Forms.

i. Put the following areas on the board:

FAMILY; HOMETOWN; SCHOOL DAYS; COLLEGE; HOLIDAYS ABROAD

ii. In pairs, students make questions to ask you about your life experience.

iii. Monitor students' work.

iv. Students ask you questions and you answer. Try to encourage students to ask follow-up questions as well.

Speaking: Other Students' Lives

i. Hand out one piece of paper per student.

ii. In pairs, students ask each other about the same areas as those on the board.

iii. Students make notes on their partners' lives. **IMPORTANT**: Students must not write the name of the person on the paper—just some information.

iv. Collect the papers in. Mix them up and redistribute so that each student has a new page.

v. Students then mingle and try to locate the person corresponding to the paper they have by asking questions of each other.

vi. When students have located the correct person, they write that student's name on the page.

vii. Feedback: Stick all the pages onto the board. Students read about each other.

3. Are You Typical?

....

Aims

i.   To give practice in the present simple tense, (especially in questions).
ii. To review adverbs of frequency.
iii. To give students practice in speaking in the context of designing and conducting a survey.

Getting Ready

This lesson does not require any special preparation.

Procedure

Warmer

Play: *What's the Topic?*

i.   Put students in small groups.
ii.   One player thinks of a kind of person (e.g. housewife, student, taxi driver).
iii. S/he says words connected to the person (e.g. laundry, homework, passengers).
iv.   Other students have to guess the kind of person with as few clues as possible.
v.   When they have guessed, another player thinks of a person and the process is repeated.
vi.   The first group to guess ten kinds of people is the winner.

NB: It's probably a good idea for you to do one with the whole class at the beginning to help them get the idea.

Vocabulary And Speaking I: Typical Stereotypes

i.   Put the following grid (or something similar) onto the board:

	Student	Housewife	Businessman	Gangster
Clothes				
Interests				
Favorite Music				
Traveling Time to Work / School				
Kind of Home				

ii.   In pairs, students come up with an entry for each category and each person.
iii. Monitor/assist as required.
iv.   Students then change partners and compare lists.
v.   For stronger groups, you might ask whether these stereotypes are fair/justified.

Speaking II: Designing A Survey

i.   Put students in pairs/small groups. Tell them they are going to design a series of questions to find out if they are typical students/businessmen/housewives.

ii.   Elicit a couple of questions from the class in order to check that everyone understands what they are expected to do.

iii. In their groups, students come up with eight questions for their survey.

iv.   Monitor/assist as required.

NB: If your students are **not** all the same kind of people (not all office workers, housewives, students etc....), have them design a questionnaire about another group. Thus, when they go to the next stage of asking the questions, they'll have people to ask!

Speaking III: Conducting A Survey

i.   Students then go and interview as many other students as possible within a given time frame (say 15 minutes).

ii.   Students come back to their first group and compare answers.

iii. Feedback: Students tell the class who they think are examples of typical students, housewives etc. …

Writing: A Typical _____

i.   Students write a short paragraph describing someone typical of a given group.

ii.   Students can do this in pairs or on their own.

iii. Monitor/assist as required.

iv.   Students swap paragraphs with another student, read and ask questions about it.

NB: If you prefer, this stage could be given as homework.

4. Describing Objects

Aims

i.   To give practice in functions for describing objects.

ii. To give students practice in speaking in the context of describing objects.

Getting Ready

This lesson requires no special preparation unless you plan to do *Warmer, Variation,* in which case you will require a piece of paper per student and some adhesive tape.

Procedure

Warmer

Play *Twenty Questions*:

i.   Put students into groups of four.

ii. One student thinks of an object (animal, vegetable or mineral).

iii. The other students have to find out what it is.

iv. The student being asked can only respond "yes," "no," "I don't know," or "it doesn't matter." The student must also tell the other players the category to which the object belongs (animal, vegetable or mineral).

v.   The three students have a limited number of questions within which they have to guess the mystery object (10 is usually sufficient).

vi. When the item is guessed, a second student thinks of something and so on round the group.

Variation

i.   Give each student a blank piece of paper.

ii. Tell students to draw an object on it.

iii. Collect in the drawings and redistribute them so that each student is allocated a picture s/he did not draw.

iv. Attach the drawings to the students' backs so that everyone else can see them.

v.   Melee: Students mingle and ask questions about the objects on their backs and try to find out what they are.

NB: Students mustn't say directly what the object on another's back is (that would obviously defeat the purpose of the exercise). If you have a very large class, have the students stick drawings on each others' backs.

Vocabulary: A Potpourri Of Objects

i.   Put the following categories on the board:

   FRUIT; TOOLS; ANIMALS; JOBS; SHOPS

ii. In pairs, students come up with five items per category.

iii. Monitor/assist as required.

iv.   Feedback: Go round the class getting one word per student until you have twenty five words on the board.

Listening: Which Object Is It?
i.   Tell students that you're going to describe one of the objects on the board.
ii.   Students listen and try to guess which one it is. When they think they know, they should raise their hand and offer an answer.
iii. Describe one or two objects in order to give students the idea.
iv.   Use the description below as a model or make up your own.

Model Listening
It's a kind of tool. It's made of metal, usually steel. You can get colorful ones but they're usually gray. It's used for tightening or loosening nuts.

(Answer: Spanner (Brit.) / Monkey Wrench (Am.))

Speaking I: The Students' Turn
i.   Put students into pairs or small groups.
ii.   Students then describe the objects on the board in similar fashion.
iii. The first group to guess five correctly is the winner.

Language Focus: Question Forms.
i.   Write the following on the board in a column:

Wood; Brown; For eating and drinking off; Quite large; Rectangular

ii.   Tell students that these are five answers.
iii. In pairs, students make up the questions which would get these answers.
iv.   Monitor/assist as required.
v.   Feedback: Get five students to come up to the board and write their answers.
Possible Questions: What's it made of?; What color is it?; What's it used for?; How big is it?; What shape is it?

Speaking II: Bilbo's Riddle (What Have I Got In My Pockets?)
i.   Tell students that you have about your person a mystery object (good objects to use are erasers, lighters...).
ii.   Students can ask you the questions from *Language Focus*, and any others they can think of in order to find out its identity.
iii. In pairs or small groups, students then continue. Each student in the group should come up with two or three objects.
iv.   The student who can guess the most correctly is the winner.

NB: You could adapt the game to include things that the students have in their homes or in their lockers (if you are teaching in a college or high school).

5. The Family

∙∙∙

Aims
i.   To give practice in the present simple tense (including question forms).
ii. To teach vocabulary relating to the family and family members.
iii. To give practice in plural and possessive *s* (Paul's sisters).
iv. To give practice in speaking and listening in the context of talking about their families.

Getting Ready
This lesson requires no special preparation although if you can arrange for students to bring in some family photos beforehand, you could use these as realia.

Procedure

Warmer

i.   Write the following on the board:

   The best age to get married is _____ because _____

   The best age to have children is _____ because _____

   A good parent should (be) _____

   A good child should (be) _____

ii. Put students into pairs or small groups.

iii. Students come up with ideas to complete the statements.

iv. Monitor/assist as required. Join in if you want.

Variation

Information Search: Put students into groups of four. Each person is responsible for one of the above four topics. Students wander around the class and find out what other people think. Students then return to their group of four and report their findings.

NB: If you do this variation, it will add about 20 minutes to the lesson time.

Vocabulary: Family Members

i.   If there is a popular TV show in the country (e.g. in Japan *Sazae-san*) have the students tell you the names of the different characters and their relationships to each other.

   e.g. Sazae is Wakame's sister etc. …

ii. Check use of target language (see: *Aims ii and iii*).

iii. Write the following on the board:

	brother's wife	
	sister's husband	
Your	mother's brother	is your ……
	aunt's daughter	
	father's mother	
	son's son	

iv.   In pairs, students complete the sentences.

v.   Feedback: Check spelling and pronunciation.

NB: If you want to teach the terms *step* and *half* you could use John Lennon and Yoko Ono and their kids, Julian, Sean and Kayoko (Yoko's daughter from her first marriage) as an example.

Listening: The Teacher's Family

i.   Tell students about four people in your family: their names, jobs, hobbies and their relationship to you.

ii.   Students listen and draw your family tree noting down the information.

iii.   Students check their work with a partner.

iv.   Retell students. Students check again.

v.   Feedback: Get two students to come up to the board and write their answers.

Speaking: The Students' Families

i.   Put students into groups of four: A, B, C, D.

ii.   Student A tells Student B about his family. Student B tells Student A.

iii.   Change partners: Student A joins Student C, Student B joins Student D.

iv.   Student A tells Student C about Student B's family. Student C takes notes. Student B tells Student D about Student A's family. Student D takes notes. Students then change roles.

v.   Student A and Student D join up. Student B and Student C join up. They check the information they got about their new partner's family from their old partner.

Variation

Instead of doing *Speaking v.* orally, students write a paragraph. The paragraph is then given to the appropriate student who reads it and checks if the information about his family is correct. This could also be a homework option.

6. What Do You Do?

∙∙

Aims
i.   To review/teach vocabulary relating to jobs.
ii. To give practice in interrogative (yes/no) questions.
iii. To develop students' knowledge of suffixes.
iv. To give speaking practice in the context of talking about jobs.

Getting Ready
This lesson requires no special preparation.

Procedure

Warmer
i.   Write on the board:

When I was a child, I wanted to be a _____ because _____

After university, I'd like to be a _____ because _____

I have/used to have a part-time job in a _____ as a _____

ii. Tell students about yourself. Encourage them to ask you questions.
iii. In pairs, students then talk about themselves.

Vocabulary: Types Of Job
i.   Put the following categories on the board:

DANGEROUS JOBS; VERY WELL-PAID JOBS; BORING JOBS;

EXCITING JOBS; JOBS WHICH REQUIRE A LOT OF STUDY.

ii. In pairs, students come up with three jobs for each category. Encourage use of dictionaries. Monitor/assist as required.
iii. Feedback: Have a few students come up to the board and write their ideas.
iv. As a class, check spelling.
v.   At this point, you could drill the students for pronunciation if you want.

Language Focus I: Suffixes
i.   Using some of the words on the board, highlight the four common endings.

e.g. dent<u>ist</u>   sing<u>er</u>   music<u>ian</u>   police<u>man</u>

ii. Tell students that these are the most common endings used for peoples' jobs. The suffix *er* is usually applied to a verb, *ist* and *an* to a noun and *man* is used for both verbs and nouns.
iii. Then write this list on the board:

bake	post	law	biology	politics
dance	police	art	manage	archaeology
act	fire	science	wait	beauty

iv. In pairs, students come up with the jobs for this list using the four suffixes. Remind them that they may need to make slight changes in spelling.

v. Feedback: Check students' efforts.

Speaking I: My Dream Job

i. Students write down on a scrap of paper a job they'd really like to do.

ii. Melee: Students walk around the room and ask each other questions about their dream job. Students cannot say directly the job they would like to do. The idea is to try and guess the dream job of as many other students as possible.

iii. The first student to guess five peoples' dream jobs is the winner.

Language Focus II: Yes/No Questions

i. Write the following on the board:

_____ your job difficult?

_____ you work with your hands?

_____ you have to wear a uniform?

_____ you need any special training?

_____ there any nice perks?

_____ you work outdoors?

ii. In pairs, students come up with one word to complete the question.

iii. Monitor/assist as required.

iv. Feedback: Get two or three students to come up to the board and write their answers.

Speaking II: Twenty Questions

i. Divide students into groups of four to six.

ii. One player thinks of a job.

iii. The other players try to guess what the job is but may only ask yes/no questions.

iv. The player who has thought of a job may only answer: "yes," "no," "maybe," "I don't know," or "it doesn't matter," in response to a question.

v. The person can be asked a maximum of ten questions. If the student defeats the guessers, he or she gets a point. If a person guesses the job correctly, he or she gets a point.

vi. The player with the most points at the end of the game is the winner.

NB: You should probably do one job yourself with the students guessing as a class in order to give them the idea.

7. Where Do You Live?

. . . .

Aims
i.   To give students practice in speaking in the context of asking for and giving directions.
ii. To give practice in the imperative.
iii. To develop lexis: places around the town.
iv. To encourage use of checking questions (Do you mean ...?/Is that ...?)

Getting Ready
This lesson requires no special preparation.

Procedure

Warmer

Ask Students: Where do you live?; Do you like your neighborhood?; What kinds of buildings are there around your house?

Vocabulary: Buildings And Facilities

i.   Put students into pairs or small groups.
ii.   Have them list the things that there are in any typical town (hospital, different kinds of shop etc. ...).
iii. Monitor/assist as required.
iv.   Feedback: Get a few of the students to come up to the board and write their ideas. Check spelling then do some work on pronunciation.

Listening : The Teacher's Home

i.   Tell students where you live, describe the general area. Tell them you are going to explain how to get to your house from your station (or bus stop). The task is for them to listen and draw a map showing the way to your home. **IMPORTANT**: Make sure that the students draw the map on a fresh piece of paper. They will (almost certainly) need the space.
ii.   Give the directions to your place. Try to keep your speech as natural as possible but try and grade your speech to the level: the higher the class, the more natural your speech.
iii. After the first listening, have students check their maps in pairs. When they have done so, give your directions again. Students then check again.
iv.   Feedback: Draw your map on the board yourself or have one of the students do it. When there is a map on the board, make any corrections that are needed and then give your directions once more. This will serve to consolidate as the students will now have an accurate visual representation to act as support.

Language Focus: Functions Of Direction

i. Write (some of) the following exponents on the board:

> Go straight; Go past the (post office); Turn left/right at the …
>
> At the end of the road, go left/right.

ii. Put students in pairs. Have them match the exponent to a point on the map where it could be used to give a direction.

iii. Monitor/assist as required.

iv. Feedback: Have students offer suggestions.

Speaking: The Students' Turn

i. Put students in pairs and if possible have them sit back to back.

ii. Students listen and draw maps from their partner's station to their house.

iii. Monitor/assist as required.

iv. Students then compare their maps with their partner. The more accurate the map, the more successfully they have completed the task.

8. Where's My Boyfriend?

Aims
i.   To review asking for and giving personal information.
ii. To review describing peoples' appearance/character.
iii. To give students practice in speaking in the context of asking and answering questions about people.

Getting Ready
Students will need a piece of paper each. If you plan to do *Warmer, Variation* you will also need an equal number of pictures of men and women.

Procedure

Warmer

i.   Tell students you've just split up with your boy/girlfriend and you're looking for a new partner!

ii. Tell students that you can no longer trust your own judgment regarding affairs of the heart and would like their help in choosing a mate.

iii. Put the following prompts on the board:

> Appearance; Personality; Hobbies; Family; Age; Job; Nationality

iv. In pairs/small groups, students come up with the perfect partner for you.

v.   Monitor/assist as required. Students may want to ask you questions.

vi. Feedback: Have the various groups tell the class your ideal person. You choose the most appropriate one. **IMPORTANT**: For conceptual continuity, it is imperative that you do select one.

Variation

i.   Put students into small groups.

ii. Distribute pictures of men and women to each group.

iii. Tell students to put the people into couples.

iv. Students discuss who goes best with whom.

v.   Monitor/assist as required.

vi. Feedback: Students explain their choices to the rest of the class. Encourage other students to ask questions.

Language Focus And Speaking I: Personal Information Questions

i.   Tell students that you love the person they've chosen for you! (see:*Warmer*).
     You're so pleased that you're going to phone your parents tonight and tell them you've found a new girl/boyfriend.

ii. Ask Students: What questions will my parents ask me about this new person?

iii. Elicit one or two questions: Where's s/he from? How old is s/he? Where did you meet? etc. …

iv. Put students into pairs/small groups. Tell them to come up with at least ten questions that your parents might ask. Let them use dictionaries.

v.   Students do task. Monitor/assist as required.

vi. Feedback: Get a few of the students to put their questions on the board. Put students in pairs and have them correct any errors.

NB: You may have to give hints e.g. whether the error is spelling, grammar, the wrong choice of word and so on.

vii. Finally, when there are correct questions on the board, do some work on pronunciation working on weak forms and intonation.

Speaking II: My Dream Partner

i. Distribute one piece of paper to each student (see: *Getting Ready*).

ii. Refer back to the prompts from *Warmer*.

iii. Put students in pairs. One student describes their dream partner to the other. The partner draws a picture of the person and under the picture make notes giving other information about them (e.g. height; hobbies; character; job).

iv. Students do task. Monitor/assist as required. **IMPORTANT**: Do not let people see the picture of their partner that is being drawn.

v. When everyone has finished, collect in all the pictures.

Speaking III: Where's My Boyfriend Got To?

i. Redistribute the pictures so that each student has neither a picture they themselves drew nor one which they described.

ii. Melee: Students mingle and have to locate their boy/girlfriend. To do this they have to ask and answer questions.

iii. When they think have found their boy/girlfriend, they take the picture and go to their partner from the previous exercise to confirm.

Speaking IV: This Is My New Boyfriend

i. Put students in new pairs.

ii. Students then (proudly) show the picture of their new boy/girlfriend to their new partner.

iii. Students then ask and answer questions about the person.

iv. Monitor/assist as required. Join in if you like.

9. Countries And Nationalities

· ·

Aims
i. To give speaking practice in the context of talking about different countries, and things for which they are well-known.
ii. To review/teach adjectives describing nationalities.
iii. To review/teach functions to talk about, describe and ask questions about different countries.
iv. To review/build lexis for describing countries.

Getting Ready
This lesson does not require any special preparation.

Procedure

Warmer

Play *A—Z game*:

i. Put students into small groups.

ii. Students go round the group naming in order countries which begin with the letters of the alphabet. (so, Student 1: Australia, Student 2: Belgium, Student 3: Canada and so on).

iii. Stress that students should try to come up with countries as fast as possible so no writing or looking at maps in their diaries).

iv. The group that can finish first is the winner.

Listening And Questioning: The Teacher's Experiences, True Or False?

i. Write up four countries on the board: e.g.

    France   Thailand   China   Indonesia

ii. Tell students that you may have been to these places or you may have not.

iii. Students have to ask you questions and through your answers judge whether you are telling the truth or lying.

iv. It's probably best to put up two countries you really have been to and two you have not. The false ones work best if they are countries that you know something about (perhaps a friend or family member has been there and told you about their holiday).

v. Answer the students' questions with as poker-a-face as you can muster.

vi. When the questions are drying up, put students in pairs and have them decide which places you've been to and which you haven't.

vii. Get one or two groups (depending on the size of the class) to give their verdicts.

viii. Tell students the answers.

Listening And Speaking I: The Students' Turn

i. Put students into small groups or pairs.

ii. Students then basically do the same (write down four countries that they may or may not have been to).

iii. Other students question (as they did you).

iv. Students then decide if their partner is telling the truth or lying.

Vocabulary: Countries, Nationalities, Places And Currency

i.   Have students write down four countries that they are interested in.

ii.   Then put the following on the board. **IMPORTANT**: Make sure you write (and have the students write) the categories in this order, left to right.

COUNTRY; NATIONALITY; LOCATION; CAPITAL CITY; CURRENCY; WEATHER

iii.   Students have to complete a table with their four countries giving the relevant information. If they're not sure, they can ask you.

iv.   Students, in pairs, help each other to complete the tables.

v.   Monitor/assist as required.

NB: You might like to do one example on the board with the whole class. e.g.

Britain; British; Off the coast of Europe; London; Pound Sterling; Wet and cold

Game: Which Country?

i.   Join pairs up to make groups of four, two teams Pair 1 and Pair 2.

ii.   Tell students that they're going to try to guess each others' four countries.

iii.   Student 1 covers up her countries revealing only the final column (weather).

iv.   The other pair have to try and guess the country from just the description of the weather.

v.   If they guess correctly, they are awarded 5 points. If they guess incorrectly, the student reveals only the next column (currency).

vi.   If the other team can now guess, they are awarded four points, if no, another column (capital city) and three points etc. …

vii.   When a country is successfully guessed, the teams change roles.

viii.   The team which has the most points at the end of the game is the winner.

ix.   Monitor/assist/adjudicate as required. Join in if you want.

NB: You may want to demonstrate this game on the board first.

Speaking II: The Best (And Worst) Of All Possible Worlds

i.   Write on the board:

A _____ house   A _____ economy

A _____ husband/wife   A _____ education

A _____ car   A _____ watch

_____ food   _____ wine

ii.   Tell students that they can choose a dream lifestyle for themselves selecting from any country in the world. Which country would they choose for each of the above categories?

iii.   In pairs, students discuss and select.
        NB: They can only choose a country once (so if they go for French food, then they can't have French wine as well).

iv.   Monitor/assist as required.
        NB: You'll probably have to teach expressions like good/bad at, famous for,

well-known for.

v.   Feedback: Have one or two pairs tell the class their choices.

Warm-Down

To end the lesson, have students repeat the process but this time devising the worst possible lifestyle, (e.g. English food, Egyptian wine, a Bulgarian watch, a North Korean economy and so on). With more advanced students you might at this point want to lead into a short discussion of stereotypes.

10. Daily Routines

Aims

i.   To give practice in the present simple tense (including question forms).
ii. To teach verbs describing everyday actions.
iii. To teach certain noun/verb collocations.
iv. To teach/review adverbs of frequency.
v.   To give practice in speaking and listening in the context of talking about one's daily routine.

Getting Ready

This lesson requires no special preparation although some flashcards of daily activities might be incorporated if you have access to them.

Procedure

Warmer

i.   Put students in pairs.

ii. Students tell each other everything they have done so far today.

iii. Students try to find four things that they both have done.

iv. Feedback: Ask one or two pairs if they found things in common.

Vocabulary: Daily Activities

i.   Write the words EVERY DAY in capitals on the board.

ii. Elicit one or two things that people do every day (e.g. wash, eat and so on).

iii. Students add to list in pairs. Encourage use of dictionaries.

iv. Monitor/assist as required.

v.   Feedback: Get two or three of the students to come up to the board and write their ideas.
     Correct spelling yourself or have students do it.
     NB: Tell them either how many spelling mistakes there are or (for weaker students) which words are spelled incorrectly.

Speaking I And Listening I: My Typical Day

i.   Tell students about your typical day, regardless of how mundane it might be! Students are generally interested in this kind of thing. There is no task as such, you are essentially modeling the next part of the lesson.

ii. Put students in pairs. Students tell each other their routines. Encourage students to ask questions.

iii. Feedback: Ask one or two students to talk (briefly) about their typical day.

Language Focus I: Collocation

i.   Write on the board:

_____ a wash	_____ dressed	_____ breakfast
_____ for work	_____ the train	_____ to work
_____ work	_____ for lunch	_____ work
_____ home	_____ changed	_____ a bath
_____ to sleep	_____ up	_____ a break

ii. Students in pairs to come up with a suitable verb for each phrase.

iii. For weaker students, put in a separate box on the board:

GET; GO; HAVE; STOP; FINISH; LEAVE; TAKE.

Students can choose from these.

Variation

This is a good opportunity to get students using their dictionaries. Most good dictionaries will give the verb that is most often found with the noun. After students have guessed a word for each blank, have them check using their dictionaries.

iv. In pairs, students then put the actions in the order in which they are usually done in the day.

v.   Students then retell their daily routine (in pairs), this time trying to use some of the expressions from the collocation exercise.

Language Focus II: Adverbs Of Frequency

i.   Write on board: Usually

ii. Ask students if they know any other words like this. Elicit a few more adverbs.

iii. Then write the following adverbs on the board and draw a series of steps. Write *always* at the top.

always; often; hardly ever; sometimes; occasionally; never; usually

iv. In pairs, students put adverbs in order on the steps.

v.   Feedback: Get one or two students to come up to the board and write their answers. Correct as necessary.

Listening II: The Teacher's Day

i. Tell students about your daily routine again.

ii. This time, be sure to use the adverbs of frequency on the board in the description.

iii. Task: Students listen and write down one activity for each adverb of frequency.

iv. Students check answers in pairs.

v. Feedback: Put correct answers on board.

vi. Students then do the same in pairs.

Language Focus III: Positioning Of Adverbs Of Frequency

i. Point out the placement of adverbs of frequency. At this level, it's probably best to tell them that the safest place to put the adverb is after the *be* verb and before other verbs.

e.g. I'm *usually* busy in the evenings. I *hardly ever* stay in on Saturday nights.

ii. Students then look back at verb/noun group from collocation exercise.

iii. Students write five sentences about themselves using that vocabulary and adverbs of frequency.

iv. Monitor/assist as required.

Speaking II: What Do I Do?

i. Get students to think of a job. **IMPORTANT**: They mustn't tell anyone what it is.

ii. Class melee: Students walk around the class and describe their daily routine without actually saying what their job is.

iii. Other students have to listen and guess what the person's job is.

iv. The first student to guess five other students' jobs is the winner.

11. People

....

Aims
i. To give practice in describing peoples' appearance and character
ii. To teach/review vocabulary for *i*.
iii. To teach/review questions: What's s/he like?; What does s/he look like?; What does s/he like doing?
iv. To give students practice in speaking and listening in the context of talking about people.

Getting Ready
This lesson requires no special preparation.

Procedure

Warmer

i.   Describe a famous person to the class. Don't say the person's name. You can use the description below or make up your own.
ii. Students listen and draw a picture of the person.
iii. In pairs, students compare drawings and try to decide who it is.
iv. Tell students the person's identity.
v.   Students then do the same in pairs.

Model Description

He's an older man, in his late sixties. He's quite tall and looks very distinguished. He's not as slim as he was when he was young, but he certainly isn't fat. His hair was once jet black but it's thinning now and going gray. He has a beard and mustache which is also gray. He's a handsome man with clear, dark-brown eyes. He has a fairly sharp nose. He's also got a strong chin. His face is quite wrinkled now but this seems to add to his character. He's a calm, intelligent-looking gentleman who you would like to have around in a crisis.

(Answer: Sean Connery)

Vocabulary: Describing People

i.   Put the following categories up on the board:

FACE; BODY; HAIR; GENERAL APPEARANCE; AGE; PERSONALITY

ii. Elicit from the class one or two words per category.
iii. Put students in pairs/small groups. Have them come up with four words for each category.
iv. Monitor/assist as required. Let students use dictionaries if they want to.
v.   Feedback: Have some of the students come up to the board and write their words for the class. Check spelling as a group (For weaker classes, tell them how many words or indeed which words are spelled incorrectly).
vi. Do some work here on pronunciation, (individual or choral drill).

Language Focus I: Be Or Have?

i.   Put the following on the board:

        She _____ a very clever girl.

        My sister _____ blue eyes.

        They _____ quite a noisy class.

        Tom and Bob both _____ long hair.

        _____ your new secretary good-looking?

        _____ your parents both got curly hair?

ii.   In pairs, students decide whether the verb *have* or *be* should be used.

iii.   Monitor/assist as required.

iv.   Feedback: Elicit answers from the class.

v.   Drill students focusing on weak forms (contractions: She is = she's etc. …).

Language Focus II: Question Forms

i.   Draw a person on the board and write up a few words describing her. e.g.

        brown hair, tall, green eyes

        friendly, intelligent

        likes tennis, reading

ii.   Elicit from students possible questions to ask in order to get the information given above. Teach the question forms:

        What does she look like?; What's she like?; What does she like doing?

iii.   Drill students focusing on liaison.

Listening: What's The Question?

i.   Assign each of the questions in *Language Focus II* a letter (A, B and C).

ii.   Tell students you're going to describe some people. They have to decide which question each description corresponds to.

iii.   Give students your descriptions. Students listen and write either A, B or C.

iv.   Students check in pairs.

v.   Tell students again. Students check again.

vi.   Tell students to listen again and make notes on the following: person's relationship to you; key description words; whether they would like to meet that person and why. Use the descriptions given below or use your own.

Model Listening

1.   My best friend at school was a boy called David. He was quite a skinny lad with blue eyes and golden hair.

2.   My favorite teacher at school was Mr. Shaddick. He was clever, had a great sense of humor and was very tolerant of us.

3.   My wife likes lots of things: cooking, flower arranging, music, but most of all she loves shopping.

4.   My new boss is a moody chap. He never smiles or says hello to you and he's rather short-tempered.

5. My mother's crazy about badminton. She plays all the time—at least three times a week. I don't see the attraction myself.

6. Our new neighbor moved in last weekend. He's quite a short guy with short curly hair and he's a bit plump.

Speaking: Let Me Introduce …

i.   Students write down the names of four people they know, two they like and two they don't. **IMPORTANT**: They mustn't indicate their relationship to that person.

ii. Melee: Students walk around the class and tell others about the people in terms of their character and personality and interests.

iii. Other students listen and try to work out if the person being described is liked or disliked by the speaker and what the relationship is.

iv. Students must speak to at least four other students in the class.

v.   The first student to have all four people guessed correctly is the winner.

12. Dates And Numbers

Aims
i.   To give practice in using dates and numbers.
ii. To teach/review prepositions of time (in May, on Monday, etc ...)
iii. To teach/review time expressions (two week's time, fortnight etc ...).
iv. To give students practice in speaking in the context of asking and answering questions about various dates and numbers.

Getting Ready
This lesson requires no special preparation.

Procedure

Warmer

i.   Get students to write down the names of four other students in the class that they know reasonably well.

ii. Then have them write down the following information about each of them:
their birthday; their phone number; their weekly income (or pocket money); how much money they have on them right now.
NB: If they don't know for sure, tell them to guess.

iii. Melee: Students then walk around the class and check their guesses/information.

Speaking I: Dates

i.   Put the following dates on the board:
> 14/07/1789; 04/07/1776; 08/12/1980; 07/12/1941 (Br.) *or*
> 07/14/1789; 07/04/1776; 12/08/1980; 12/07/1941 (Am.)

ii. Ask students how to say the above dates
Teach: month+(the)+date+year e.g. July (the) fourteenth, 1789
NB: At this level, it's probably better not to teach the expression: *the fourteenth of July*. Point out the difference between American English, which tends to place the month first, and British English which tends to place the date first.

iii. In pairs, students try to work out what happened on these dates in history.

iv. Feedback: Have one or two students come up to the board and write their answers, then give students the correct answers.
(Answers: The storming of the Bastille (French Revolution); The U.S. Declaration of Independence; The death of John Lennon; The attack on Pearl Harbor by the Japanese Imperial Navy).

Vocabulary I And Speaking II: Dates And Time Expressions

i. Write the following questions on the board:

What's the date today?

When's the next national holiday?

What was the date the day before yesterday?

What's the day after tomorrow's date?

When's your partner's birthday?

When was the last national holiday?

When's your father's birthday?

What's the date this Sunday?

What's the date in a fortnight's time?

What's the date a week from Sunday?

ii. Students, in pairs, answer the questions. Monitor/assist as required. Let them use dictionaries if they need to.

iii. Feedback: Have some of the students come up to the board and write their answers. Get the class to say the dates (choral drill).

Vocabulary II And Language Focus: Days, Months And Prepositions

i. Get students (in pairs) to write the seven days of the week and the twelve months of the year.

ii. While they are doing that, write up the following on the board:

Tom was born ____ a Sunday ____ 6:45 ____ the evening.

We're going to France ____ July.

My parents came to visit ____ the weekend.

Shakespeare died ____ 1616.

We had a meeting ____ Tuesday.

I want to go ____ holiday ____ Christmas.

I brush my teeth ____ the morning and also ____ night.

iii. Check students know the days of the week/months of the year. Then, in pairs, students try to complete the sentences above with a suitable preposition.

iv. Monitor/assist as required.

v. Feedback: Get a few students to write their answers on the board.

NB: You could then give students this guideline to follow when deciding which preposition to use: Dates take *on*; Days take *on*; Months take *in*; Years take *in*; Exact time takes *at*; Periods of time take *in*; Events such as Christmas, the Olympics, Easter etc. ... are in a sense, exact points in time and therefore take *at*.

Listening: Numbers In Context

i. Tell students you're going to make a series of statements each containing a number. Students have to listen and note down only the number.

ii. Make the statements below (or adapt them if you prefer).

iii. Students listen and note down the numbers and check with their partner.

iv.   Repeat statements. Students listen and check again.

v.   Feedback: Have one or two students come up to the board and write their answers.

vi.   Tell Ss to listen again. This time, students have to listen and note down what the number refers to.
      NB: Just the main point, not verbatim.

vii. Feedback: Get the students answers. Correct as required.

Model Listening

1.   Paul usually takes the number 228 bus to get to work.

2.   Japan's population is about 125,000,000.

3.   Leap years have an extra day so they have a total of 366.

4.   Last year, the workers got a pay rise of 4.7%.

5.   The Concorde can travel from Europe to America in about two and a half hours.

6.   The starting salary for an office worker in Japan is about ¥165,000 a month.

7.   About 200 languages and dialects are spoken in India.

8.   The Sun is about 93,000,000 miles from the Earth.

Speaking III: How Much?

i.   Put students in pairs and write the following on the board.

ii.   Students discuss and estimate the cost of the items below.

iii. Feedback: Get a class consensus for the items' cost.

	dinner for two in a nice restaurant	
	a new pair of lady's shoes	
How much is:	a second-hand four-door saloon	in your country?
	a brand-new four-door saloon	
	a three-bedroom house	
	a daily tabloid newspaper	

Writing And Speaking IV: Here's The Price, What Is It?

i.   In pairs, students write in words the cost of five things in their countries.
      IMPORTANT: They must not write down the name of the item itself.

ii.   Monitor/assist as required. Help with any vocabulary problems.

iii. Melee: Students then mingle and dictate the numbers to other students who must write down the figure in numbers not words.

iv.   The student then tries to guess what the number is the cost of. The student whose number is being guessed is allowed to give hints if the guesser is having difficulty but may not say outright what the mystery item is.

v.   The first student to have all five figures that s/he wrote down guessed, is the winner.

vi.   Monitor/assist as required. Join in if you want.

13. Comparatives

Aims
i. To give practice in the comparative form of adjectives.
ii. To teach/review structure: as … as …
iii. To give students practice in speaking in the context of comparing people and places.

Getting Ready
This lesson requires no special preparation unless you plan to do *Warmer Variation*, in which case you will need some pictures of people.

Procedure

Warmer

i. Tell students to get in a line: the youngest at one end, the oldest at the other, e.g.

X	X	X	X	X	X
18	19	25	28	31	46

ii.   When students are in a line, have them name someone they are older than and younger than. (e.g. I'm older than Pierre and younger than Keiko and so on).

NB: If you are teaching in a high school or university where students are in the same academic year, this works even better as they'll have to be precise about birthdays. If you have a very large class (30-40 students), divide the class into three or four groups for this activity.

Variation

i.   Put students in groups and give each group a few pictures (see: *Getting Ready*).
ii.   In their groups, students have to come up with as many differences between the people as they can.
iii.   Monitor/assist as required.
iv.   Feedback: Have the groups show the pictures to the class and explain the differences.

Language Focus I: Comparatives

i.   Draw three people on the board and give the following information:

John	Sally	Robert
17	22	31
1.60m.	1.54m.	1.60m.
65 kg.	65 kg.	72 kg.

ii.   Ask students to make comparisons about the people.
iii.   Elicit the following:

John is younger than Sally.   John is as tall as Robert.
Sally is shorter than Robert.   Sally is as heavy as John.
Robert is heavier than John.   Sally is not as tall as John.

iv. Drill students (chorally and individually), then elicit yes/no question forms
     (Is ... taller than ...? etc. ...).

Listening I: Me And My Family

i.   Tell students you're going to compare members of your family with yourself.
     NB: You can use the model given below as a guide.
ii. Students listen and write down any comparatives they hear.
iii. Students listen and note down comparatives, then check with a partner.
iv. Tell students again. This time students have to decide whether the word refers to you or a
     member of your family. (e.g. "I'm taller than my mother" refers to you. "My sister isn't
     as clever as me" refers to you).
v.   Students listen again and make notes, then check in pairs.
vi. Feedback: Have one or two students come up to the board and write their answers.

Model Listening

I'm quite a bit taller than my mother but she's not as heavy as I am. My sister isn't as clever as me that's for
sure, but she's a much better driver. She's never had an accident but I've had four or five. My brother is older
than me, by about eight years but I'm much more handsome than he is.

Speaking I: The Students' Turn

i.   Put students in pairs. Have them come up with differences between themselves
     and their own family members as you did.
ii. Monitor/assist as required. Join in if you like. Encourage questions.
iii. Feedback: Students change pairs and tell their new partner about their old partner.

Language Focus II: Making The Comparative Form

i.   Put the following three words on the board:

         young   heavy   expensive

ii. Elicit the comparative forms: younger, heavier, more expensive.
iii. Ask students if they know the rule for making the form. Teach the rule.
     NB: At this level, it's probably not a good idea to go into spelling rules. Keep it simple:
              a. short words (one sound only): add *er*
              b. 'y' words (ending in 'y'): drop the 'y' and add *ier*
              c. long words (more than one sound): add *more*
iv. Put up a list of adjectives on the board
              young, old, narrow, short, pretty, ugly, good, bad, peaceful, modern, safe, dangerous,
              wide, smooth, rough.

v.   In pairs, students write the comparative form applying the above rule.
vi. Feedback: Get some of the students to come up to the board and write their answers.
vii. Check for any spelling mistakes and then do some work on pronunciation.

Listening II And Speaking II: Can You Guess What It Is?

i.   Tell students you're going to describe something and they have to try and guess what it is.

ii.   Describe something (an animal, a fruit, an object).

NB: You can use the examples given below or make up your own if you prefer.

iii. Students listen. When a student knows what it is, s/he raises her hand and says.

iv.   Do this a couple of times to give students the idea of the game.

v.   Put students in small groups. One student describes an object, the others have to guess.

vi.   The first group to guess ten objects is the winner.

Model Listening

1.   It's smaller than a dining table, but bigger than a chair. It's got more legs than a person but fewer than a spider. It's heavier than a baby but not as heavy as a desk.   (Answer: coffee table)

2.   It's taller than an elephant but not as strong. It can run faster than a dog but not as fast as a deer. It's neck is longer than a bush but shorter than a tree.   (Answer: giraffe)

Speaking III: How Many Differences?

i.   Write on board:

        credit cards vs. cash

        living at home vs. living on your own

        a holiday abroad vs. a holiday in your own country

        your hometown vs. the place you're living in now

        a Rolls Royce vs. a Mini

        going to the cinema vs. renting a video

        your present boy/girlfriend vs. your last one

ii.   In pairs, students have to come up with four differences for each of the pairs.
      e.g. living at home is cheaper, a holiday abroad is more exciting etc. …

iii. Monitor/assist as required.

iv.   Feedback: Get one or two pairs to tell the class their ideas.

14. Hotels

....

Aims
i.   To review/teach vocabulary relating to hotels.
ii. To give practice in checking-in and asking for information at a hotel.
iii. To give practice in speaking in the context of discussing preferences in hotels.

Getting Ready
This lesson requires no special preparation.

Procedure

Warmer

i.   Put students in pairs.

ii.   Students have to come up with five different types of hotel (e.g. a five-star hotel;
      a youth hostel; a boarding house and so on) and list how they are similar or different.

iii. Monitor/assist as required.

iv.   Have one or two pairs tell the class their ideas. Keep it short though!

Vocabulary I And Speaking I: My Preferences

i.   Put the following on the board:

near the beach _____   friendly staff _____   24-hour room service_____

a sauna_____   a gym_____   fax and telex facilities_____

reasonable rates _____   a pool _____   a variety of restaurants_____

ii.   Tell students that they and their partner are going on holiday together. Students have
      to rank the items in terms of importance (1 = most, 9 = least).

iii. Monitor/assist as required.

iv.   Feedback: Get one or two pairs to tell the class their opinion.

NB: With stronger groups, you could elicit the different kinds of facilities and services first and use
those instead of the ones given above.

Vocabulary II: People, Places, Things To Do

i.   Put the following categories on the board:
      PEOPLE; PLACES; THINGS TO DO

ii.   Elicit one or two examples from the class for items in each category (bellboy, lobby,
      check in/out).

iii. In pairs, students then continue adding to the categories.

iv.   Monitor/assist as required. Let students use dictionaries if they want to.

v.   Feedback: Get two or three students to come up to the board and write their ideas.
      Check spelling and do some work on pronunciation (choral/individual drill).

Language Focus: Checking-In And Asking Questions

i. Write the following dialogue on the board:

Receptionist	**Guest**
Good morning sir. Can I help you?	Oh. I'm rather hungry actually.
Just a moment please, sir. Is that Robert Willis of Toronto?	Thanks very much.
That's fine sir. Could you just fill in the form and sign the register please.	Thanks. Is there a restaurant in the hotel?
Thanks very much. I'll have a porter take your luggage up to your room.	Yes. I have a reservation in the name of Willis.
There is sir, but I'm afraid we don't start serving lunch until 11:45.	Thank you. Where is she?
There's always room service. We could do you some toasted sandwiches, or an omelet if you like.	That's right. I booked a single room for two nights.
Yes sir. If you'd like to contact our business liaison officer, she'll be more than happy to help you.	Of course. Could I borrow a pen?
Past the elevators, first door on the left, sir.	Okay. That's fine.
Not at all sir. Here's your key and I hope you enjoy your stay.	And I need to fax my office. Do you have a machine in the hotel?

ii.   Tell students that the receptionist's part of the dialogue is in the correct order, but the guest's is mixed up.

iii. Students in pairs draw lines connecting the speakers' utterances so that the conversation makes sense.

iv.   Monitor/assist as required.

v.   Feedback: Get one pair to come up to the board and draw their answer.

vi: Get students then to practice the dialogue in pairs.

vii. Monitor/assist as required. Help with intonation.

viii. Feedback: Have one or two pairs perform the dialogue for the class.

Speaking II: Where Shall I Stay?

i. Divide class into two and put students into pairs (So: 20 students = two groups of five pairs each).

ii. Group 1 are hoteliers, Group 2 are travelers.

iii. The hoteliers have to invent the following for their hotel: name; location; price per night; types or room available; facilities. The travelers have to invent the following: what kind of room they need; any particular facilities they need/want; how much they can afford.

iv. Monitor/assist as required.

   NB: Try to ensure that students inject a certain amount of realism into their work.
   e.g. a student traveling on a budget could not afford a $200-dollar-a-night hotel!

v. Game: Travelers then go around to all the different hotels and try to find the one which best suits their needs by asking the hoteliers about their respective hotels.

vi. The hoteliers who get the most clients are the winners.

15. Superlatives

Aims
i.   To give practice in the superlative form of adjectives.
ii. To give students practice in speaking in the context of doing a quiz.
iii. To give students practice in listening in the context of checking and confirming guesses.
iv. To review the comparative form of adjectives.

Getting Ready
Students will need a copy of the quiz each.

Procedure

Warmer

i.   Write the following questions on the board:

> What's the smallest thing in your bag?
>
> What's the hottest place you've ever been to?
>
> What's the longest land journey you've ever made?
>
> What was your most difficult subject at school?
>
> What's the most expensive gift you've ever given?

ii. Melee: Students walk around and talk to six other students and note down their answers to the above questions.
iii. Monitor/assist as required.
iv. Put students in pairs. Students report their findings to their partner.
v.   Feedback: Have one or two students tell the class the most interesting answer they got. **NB**: Keep it brief!

Listening I: The Teacher's Answers

i.   Tell students you're going to answer the same questions but NOT in the order that they're written on the board. Students have to listen, work out which question you're answering and then note down your answer.
ii. Tell students your answers (you can use the model below as a guide if you like).
iii. Students listen, make notes and check their answers with a partner.
iv. Tell students again. Students check again.
v.   Have three or four students come up to the board and write their answers. Check students' work.

Model Listening

I really didn't like chemistry. I couldn't understand what any of the symbols meant or even why we were studying it. I always came bottom in tests.

My fiancee's engagement ring, definitely. It cost about $5,000 and it really hurt to hand over that much cash!

Several years ago, I went to the deserts of north-west India. The temperature there was about 43 degrees centigrade.

I have a lucky charm that I always carry with me which I bought at a temple in southern Japan. It's supposed to keep you healthy.

Again, when I was in India, I traveled from the south right up to the Nepal border overland. That's a distance of about 1,000 miles.

Language Focus I: Reviewing The Comparative

i. Draw three people on the board and give the following information:

John	Sally	Robert
17	22	31
1.60m.	1.54m.	1.60m.
65 kg.	65 kg.	72 kg.

ii. Ask students to make comparisons about the people.

iii. Elicit the following:

John is younger than Sally.

Sally is shorter than Robert.

Robert is heavier than John.

John is as tall as Robert.

Sally is as heavy as John etc. …

iv. Drill students (chorally and individually), then elicit yes/no question forms:

Is … taller than …? and so on.

v. Then point to Robert and have students compare him to the other two.

Elicit: Robert is the tallest. Repeat for shortest, youngest, oldest, heaviest, lightest.

Language Focus II: Making The Superlative Form

i. Put the following three words on the board:

young   heavy   expensive

ii. Elicit the superlative forms: youngest, heaviest, most expensive.

iii. Ask students if they know the rule for making the form. Teach the rule.

NB: At this level, it's probably not a good idea to go into spelling rules. Keep it simple:

a. short words (one sound only): add *est*

b. 'y' words (ending in 'y'): drop the 'y' and add *iest*

c. long words (more than one sound): add *most*

NB: Remind/teach students that the superlative always takes the definite article (the).

iv. Put up a list of adjectives on the board:

young, old, narrow, short, pretty, ugly, good, bad, peaceful, modern, safe, dangerous, wide, smooth, rough

v. In pairs, students write the superlative form applying the above rule.

vi. Feedback: Get some of the students to come up to the board and write their answers.

vii. Check for any spelling mistakes and then do some work on pronunciation.

Speaking I: The World Of Records

i.   Hand out a copy of the worksheet to each student (see: *Getting Ready*).

ii.   In pairs, students try to come up with an answer for each question.
      IMPORTANT: It's very unlikely that students will actually know the answers
      given the nature of the questions. This is a chance to have them speculate and discuss.

iii. Melee: Have students mingle and check each answer with a different student (so they
      have to talk to thirteen other students).

iv.   Students go back into their pairs, report what they learned and decide whether
      to amend their guesses based on what they heard.

Listening II: The Answers

i.   Tell students you're going to give them the answers. They have to listen and note
      them down.

ii.   Students listen/note down answers and check with a partner.

iii. Tell students again. Students listen and check again.
      (Answers: Nepal; Japan; cheetah; Glyn Wolfe, a Baptist priest, 27 times; 59cm; 2.64m;
      Japan; 1.3 seconds; 592; get married; 4032; chess; 141,078)

NB: The answers given above are in the order in which they appear on the worksheet (so you'll
know the correct answers). For the listening exercise you will have to give them to the students in a
different order.

Speaking II: Mix And Match

i.   Put students into small groups.

ii.   Students look at the answers and try to match them to the correct question.

iii. Monitor/assist as required.

iv.   Feedback: Give students the correct answers.

WORKSHEET FOR SUPERLATIVES

Where is the highest capital city in Asia?

Which is bigger, Japan or Britain?

Which is the world's fastest land mammal?

Who has been married the most number of times? What is his/her job? How many times has he/she been married?

What was the height of the shortest person ever?

What was the height of the tallest person ever?

Which country has the oldest national anthem?

Steven Petrosino (USA) drank the fastest liter of beer. How fast did he drink?

How many people did the world's greatest killer murder?

Harry Stevens, at 103 years of age, is the oldest person to do what?

How many rooms are there in the world's largest hotel?

Which is the world's oldest board game?

Chamoy Thipyaso is serving the longest ever prison sentence. How many years does she have to stay in jail for before being set free?

(Information gathered from *The Guiness Book of World Records*, 1997)

16. Describing A Room

Aims
i. To teach/review vocabulary relating to rooms and furniture.
ii. To teach/review prepositions of location.
iii. To give practice in the present simple tense (including question forms).
iv. To give practice in speaking and listening in the context of describing a room.

Getting Ready
Some flashcards of rooms and furniture would help the lesson but they are not essential.

Procedure

Warmer

i. Put students in pairs and have them explain to each other three things they like and three things they dislike about their house.

ii. Feedback: Get one or two of the students to tell the class.

Vocabulary: Kinds Of Furniture

i. Draw a house on the board. Elicit the names of different rooms in the house.
    e.g. living room, bedroom, study, kitchen

ii. Divide class into groups of three or four. Allocate one room to each group.

iii. In their group, students have to come up with different furniture found in their room. Let them use dictionaries or ask you.

iv. Monitor students. Help with spelling.

v. Mix up members to make new groups. Each student explains/teaches their words to the other members.

Variation

Have students come up with some definitions for their words. Students give their definitions and other students have to guess the item.

    e.g. You sleep in it at night. (Answer: bed)

NB: If you do this version, it will add about 30 minutes to the lesson.

Listening: The Teacher's Room

i. Draw the outline of your room on the board.

ii. Tell students that you're going to describe the contents of your room to them and where they can be found. Students have to listen and draw in the furniture according to your description.

iii. Tell students.
    NB: It would be wise to rehearse this before the lesson. Adjust your speech to take account of the students' level but try to speak naturally (include liaison, weak forms etc.).

iv. When you finish, students check their rooms in pairs. Retell students and they check again.

v.   Have one or two students come up to the board and fill in the outline of your room on the board.

vi. Correct any mistakes.

Language Focus: Prepositions Of Location

i.   Write up some true/false sentences on the board based on your room. e.g.

    The bed's against the wall.

    The TV's between the coffee table and the desk.

ii. Students have to identify those which are true and then correct the remainder so that all the sentences on the board are true.

    NB: Focus the true/false item on prepositions of location rather than lexical items.

iii. Feedback: Correct students' efforts.

Speaking: Drawing Your Partner's Room

i.   Put students into pairs.

ii. Student A listens to Student B and draws his/her room.

iii. Students then reverse roles.

iv. Monitor assist as required.

v.   Feedback: Students check each others' drawings.

Variations

i.   For very low level classes, have students draw the contents of their own room. Students then exchange pictures. Their partner then draws in some spiders into their partner's room. Students have to try and locate the spiders in their room.

ii. For stronger groups, students can plan a dream house or room.

17. The Past

Aims
i.   To give practice in use of the past tense especially in questions.
ii. To give speaking practice in the context of designing and playing a quiz about famous past events.
iii. To give practice in use of weak forms.

Getting Ready
This lesson requires no special preparation.

Procedure

Warmer

i.   Write a telephone number on the board: e.g.

   3931-1266

ii. Tell students it was your phone number when you were at college or as a child.

iii. Divide the number into pairs. So: 39 37 12 66

iv. Ask students if they can think of any famous events which happened in these years in any century. Most students should be able to come up with something.

   e.g. 39 (start of W.W.II 1939)

   31 (Japan's invasion of China 1931)

   12 (the defeat of Napoleon 1812)

   66 (The Battle of Hastings 1066)

v.   In pairs/small groups, students contribute one or two phone numbers each and try to come up with some more famous events.

Dictation: Writing Questions

i.   Tell students to write down the following five questions exactly. Speak naturally (using weak forms and liaison etc. …) but adjust your speed according to the level of the class. Use the questions provided or make your own. It depends a lot on your students' general knowledge.

   1.   When and where was Kennedy assassinated? (Dallas, 1963)

   2.   When was the Great Fire of London? (1666)

   3.   When did Hong Kong go back to Chinese rule? (July 1st, 1997)

   4.   What happened to Nagasaki in 1945? (It was hit by an A-Bomb)

   5.   When did the Berlin Wall fall? (1989)

ii. Repeat each question twice. Students listen and try to write down what you say.

iii. Students check their work in pairs after each question.

iv. Finally, repeat all five questions one last time.

v.   Have five students come up to the board and write one question each.

vi. Students in pairs try to answer questions.

vii. Feedback: Give correct answers.

Speaking And Writing: Designing And Playing A Quiz

i. Divide class into teams of four players.

ii. Each team has to come up with five questions of their own about either their country's or world history.

iii. Monitor students, help with spelling and problem vocabulary.

iv. Play: *History Game.* Team A asks a question, the other teams listen. First team to raise a hand has the first chance to answer the question. If they answer correctly, they get five points but if they answer incorrectly, three points are deducted and another team has the chance to answer. Team B then asks a question. Same rules apply. The team which scores the most points is the winner.

18. Storytelling

Aims
i. To give practice in using narrative tenses.
ii. To give speaking practice in the context of telling a story.
iii. To give listening practice in the context of reproducing a picture.
iv. To give writing practice in the context of telling a story.

Getting Ready
Students will need two pieces of paper each. Adhesive tape or Blue Tack would also be useful (see: *Reading*).

Procedure

Warmer

i. Hand out one piece of paper to each student.

ii. Tell them you're going to describe a scene to them. They listen and draw a picture.

iii. Describe a scene to the students. Try to include some interesting details and some unusual action. Below is one I have often used with good results. You can adapt this or make up one yourself.

iv. Students listen and draw a picture, then check with a partner.

v. Tell students again. Students (try to) improve their work.

vi. Draw the correct picture on the board.

Model Listening

In the background are some rolling hills. It's a beautiful sunny day with the sun shinning in the left of the picture. There are three birds flying from left to right across the picture. At the foot of the hills is a small cottage, the sort of house you might find in the English countryside. There is smoke coming from the chimney and there's a cat sitting on the roof. The house has four windows, two upstairs, two downstairs. The upstairs right-hand window is open and a small girl of about seven or eight is looking out at something. In front of the house is a small pond. The water is quite shallow and there are three large stones in the pond touching the surface of the water. On one of the stones is a frog sitting with his tongue shooting out. He's about to catch a fly for his lunch. Next to the pond is a group of three people all of whom are dressed very formally, two men and a woman. The woman is sitting down in the center and is playing the cello. The man to her right, an older chap in his sixties, is playing the accordion. The man to her left is much younger, about twenty five. He's playing the trumpet.

Speaking And Listening: The Students' Drawings

i. Students turn over the page.

ii. In Pairs: Student A describes a scene of his/her own, Student B draws it, then vice-versa.

iii. Students then check each others' drawings.

iv. Students then draw their partner into the picture doing something. Stress to students that they can be as cruel or as kind as they like! Students then give the picture to their partner.

Writing I: Telling A Story

i.   Explain to students that the drawing they have is a picture of something they were doing last weekend.

ii.   Hand out the second piece of paper.

iii. On the new sheet, students have to write a paragraph explaining what they were doing, where they were and why they were doing it. Set a time limit of about 10-15 minutes for this.

iv.   Monitor/assist as required.

v.   Collect in all the drawings and paragraphs.

Reading: Which Picture? Which Story?

i.   Mix up the drawings and redistribute so that each student has a completely new picture. (Neither one s/he drew nor described).

ii.   Stick the students' paragraphs around the room at random. (If you do not have any tape, you can place them on surfaces such as desks, your table, or even the floor).

iii. Students wander round the class reading the paragraphs until they find the one that corresponds to the picture they have been given. When they have found the paragraph, they should collect it and sit down.

Writing II: Asking Questions And Rewriting

i.   Students read the paragraph again. This time they have to come up with at least five questions to ask about the story in order to get more information or detail.

ii.   As students do this, monitor and assist. You will probably need to prod the students a bit as this kind of open question format may be new to them.

iii. When they have written their questions, students give both picture and paragraph to its author.

iv.   The student then reads the questions and must rewrite his/her paragraph so that the questions are answered.

v.   The rewritten paragraph is then returned to the questioner who reads it and is (we hope) satisfied.

19. What About This Weekend?

....

Aims

i. To develop vocabulary for describing freetime activities.
ii. To practice collocations of above with play/go/do.
iii. To give practice in using future forms (esp. going to ...; might ...; will probably ...).
iv. To give practice in speaking and listening in the context of talking about the coming weekend.

Getting Ready

This lesson requires no special preparation unless you plan to do *Warmer, Variation 2*.

Procedure

Warmer

i. In pairs, students talk about their plans for the coming weekend. Students try and find two things in common that they are both planning to do.

Variation 1

i. Class Melee: Students walk around the room and try to find something in common with as many other students as possible within a given time period (10 minutes?).

ii. Feedback: Students return to their seats and tell the person next to them what they found out.

Variation 2

i. *Find the Lie*: Prepare slips of paper with a range of events on them,
    e.g. buy a pair of boots; go to a rock concert; visit a museum

ii. Give each student a slip of paper. They have to tell their partner about their plans for the coming weekend and must include in the description the event that you have given them. Their partner listens and tries to guess which event is written on the slip.

Vocabulary: Hobbies And Activities

i. Elicit from class a few examples of things people do **for fun** at the weekend.

ii. In pairs, students continue working on their list.

iii. Monitor/assist as required.

iv. Then write on board:
    PLAY; GO; DO

v. With their partner, students put the items they have come up with under the correct verb. You may need to give one or two examples to help them get the idea.

vi. Have one or two students come up to the board and write some examples.

vii. Try to elicit the rule regarding the use of the three verbs. (The basic rule is: *play* is used when the activity requires more than one person, *go* is used when you are using a gerund (ing) form and *do* is used with violent, contact sports (boxing, kung fu ...) or activities done especially for health (yoga, aerobics etc. ...).

Listening: The Teacher's Weekend

i.   Tell students about your own plans for the coming weekend. Make sure you use the target language forms (see: *Aims iii*).

ii. Draw three columns on the board with the following headings:

SURE; GOOD CHANCE; SMALL CHANCE

iii. Have students copy down these three columns.

iv. Students listen to your plans for the weekend and fill in activities under each column.

v.   Students check with a partner. You then retell them. Students check again.

vi. Have two or three students come up to the board and write their answers

Language Focus: Future Forms

i.   Write three sentences on the board:

I'm going to the cinema on Friday.

I'll probably go for a swim on Saturday morning.

I might write some letters on Sunday.

ii. In pairs, students match the degree of possibility (sure, good chance, small chance) with the appropriate sentence.

iii. Feedback: Check students' efforts.

Speaking I: The Students' Weekends

i.   In pairs (with a new partner if possible), students talk again about their plans for the weekend. This time they should think carefully about the likelihood of actually doing the activities.

ii. Partner listens and makes notes under the same three headings as in the listening exercise.

iii. Students then change partners and report about their old partner's plans.

Speaking II: Guess What I'm Doing

i.   Students write down the names of four other students in the class.

ii. For each student, they have to guess what they're doing at the weekend. They should come up with one activity for each of the three options: sure; good chance; small chance (so 12 activities altogether).

iii. Students mingle and check their predictions with the four students (I think you might have lunch with your girlfriend on Saturday etc. …).

NB: You could if you like make a game out of it; the person who guesses the most correctly is the winner, the person who guesses the least has to pay some kind of forfeit.

20. Wordbuilding I

Aims
i.   To develop range of adjectives.
ii. To give practice in speaking in the context of creating a dialogue.
iii. To develop strategies for dealing with unknown words.

Getting Ready
Each pair of students will require a piece of paper.

Procedure

Warmer

i.   Write the following on the board:

   It's a _____ day today, isn't it?

   What a _____ coat that is!

   I think our teacher is a really _____ person.

   London (or a more relevant city) is such an _____ city.

   Mexican food is _____ .

ii. In pairs, students come up with two possibilities for each space.
     NB: They can't repeat words so ten words altogether.

iii. Feedback: Get some of the students to tell you their words.

Vocabulary I: Twenty Words As Fast As You Can!

i.   Divide class into teams of 4—6 players.

ii.   Divide the board so that each team has a piece of board.

iii. One team member comes up from each team and writes numbers 1—20 vertically in two columns (1—10, and 11—20).

iv.   The team has to come up with 20 adjectives (words like the ones in *Warmer*, you could tell them). Members call out words, the player at the board acts as secretary for the whole team.

v.   Students cannot repeat a word in another team's list. So if Team A has already got *interesting* for example, Team B may not use it.

vi.   The team that can finish first is the winner.

vii. Feedback: Get the class to look at all the words on the board and check spelling.

Vocabulary II: Words I Want To Learn

i.   Students (individually) choose (from any of the words on the board) three words for each of the following categories:

   NEW WORDS; WORDS I LIKE; PARTICULARLY USEFUL WORDS

ii.   In pairs, students then compare the nine words they have chosen. How many are the same/different?

iii.	Students then pool their words (= up to 18 words). Using their dictionaries, students come up with words which have the opposite meaning.

iv.	Monitor assist as required.

NB: Try to get students to find completely new words where possible rather than just using a prefix (So, for example: happy/sad **NOT** happy/unhappy).

Speaking And Writing: Preparing A Dialogue

i.	Put the following situations on the board:

Two strangers on a train	At the beach
At a baseball/football game	In a bar
In the office	Two strangers on a plane

ii.	Students in pairs choose one of the topics.

iii.	Students then write a short dialogue which must include eight of the words they selected from the vocabulary exercise.

> **NB**: They can choose from the opposites too.

iv.	In pairs, students write dialogue. Monitor/assist as required.

v.	Feedback: Each pair performs their dialogue for another pair. The listeners must guess which topic it is that they have written about.

vi.	Get one or two of the more interesting dialogues performed for the whole class.

Warm-Down: Password

i.	Hand out one piece of paper per pair (see: *Getting Ready*).

ii.	Have students tear it into 16 pieces.

iii.	On each separate piece, students write one word (so 16 words altogether).

iv.	Monitor/assist with spelling.

v.	Have students then put all 16 words in one neat pile face-down.

vi.	Rotate the piles round one pair so that each pair has another pair's words.

> **NB**: It's probably quicker and more efficient to do the rotation yourself than have the students do it.

vii.	Play: *Password*. One student takes a word and does not show it to his partner. S/he describes the word but does not say it directly. The partner listens and tries to guess the word.

viii.	When s/he guesses the word, s/he takes a second word and the process is repeated.

iv.	The pair which guesses all 16 words correctly first is the winner.

NB: It's probably best to demonstrate the game yourself with one of the stronger students. Do this by having the student face the class and you writing a word on the board so that everyone in the class can see the word except for the student doing the guessing.

21. A Weekend Away

· ·

Aims
i.   To review functions of suggestion, giving opinions, agreeing and disagreeing.
ii. To review/teach vocabulary relating to freetime activities.
iii. To give practice in speaking in the context of planning a weekend away.

Getting Ready
This lesson requires no preparation.

Procedure

Warmer

i.   In pairs, students talk about what they did last weekend.
ii. Task: Students try and find three things they both did.
iii. Monitor/assist as required.
iv. Feedback: Ask one or two pairs if they found things in common.

Vocabulary: Things We Do for Fun

i.   Brainstorm things that people do at the weekend for fun.
ii. Put the three areas below onto the board:

> AT HOME; IN TOWN; OUT OF TOWN

iii. Get students to come up with a range of activities that can be done in these three
     places.
     NB: You might like to demonstrate and encourage the use of mind maps as a way of
     storing vocabulary for this exercise.
iv. Monitor/assist as required. Let students use their dictionaries if they want to.
v.   Feedback: Get one or two students to come up to the board and write their ideas.

Speaking I: Planning A Weekend Away

i.   Put students in pairs or small groups.
ii.   Allocate students a very small sum of money. The amount should be determined
      by the place where the students are living (e.g. Tokyo students, ¥20,000 per pair,
      in London £150 per pair, New York, $200 per pair).
iii. Students have to plan a weekend away using only this money. They have to leave the
      city/town on Friday night and cannot come back until Sunday evening.
iv.   No credit cards or loans from parents can be entertained!
v.   Pairs come up with a weekend plan. Monitor/assist as required.
vi.   Regroup students (so Students A1 & A2 & B1 & B2 = A1 & B1 & A2 & B2).
vii. Students tell their new partner their plan for the weekend. The partner listens and
      challenges if s/he thinks that something is unfeasible (e.g. "Two return tickets to Osaka
      cost ¥6,000." "No way!").
viii. The pair which has the most interesting weekend away within the budget is the winner.

Language Focus: Suggesting, Agreeing, Disagreeing

i. Write dialogues similar to the following on the board:

_____ going to Hakone for the weekend?

_____ . I've never been there before.

_____ visiting Sendai?

_____ . It'll cost too much and it's not very
interesting.

_____ rent a car and drive into the countryside?

_____ but I don't think there's enough money for
that.

ii. In pairs, students come up with possible phrases for the spaces.

iii. Monitor/assist as required.

iv. Feedback: Get one or two students to come up top the board and write their ideas.

v.   Check Students efforts. Correct as necessary.

vi. Do some drilling here focusing on intonation.

NB: For weaker students, you can put choices on the board for them to choose from. e.g.
how about, what about, why don't we, that's a good idea, I don't think so, I'd like to.

The places given above are based on my own teaching location. Adapt the dialogues according
to where you are.

Speaking II: My Dream Weekend

i. This works more or less as the first speaking exercise except that this time, students
have an enormous amount of money. You could tell them that they found it on the
street or something like that. Allocate perhaps ¥500,000, £3,000 or $5,000.

ii. Monitor students and encourage use of target language.

22. Scar Stories

Aims
i.   To give students practice in speaking in the context of narration.
ii. To give practice in a variety of past forms (simple, continuous, perfect).
iii. To develop vocabulary: parts of the body, medical terms
     (illnesses, hospital, bandage etc. …).
iv. To develop vocabulary relating to feelings.

Getting Ready
Each pair of students will require one piece of paper each (see: *Rotation Writing*).

Procedure

Vocabulary: Mind Maps

i.   Write the word SCAR on the board.

ii. Put students into groups or pairs. Brainstorm related vocabulary. Encourage students to come up with anything. Tell them you're not looking for any words in particular. You'll probably have to give a few examples yourself first before they get the idea.

iii. Monitor/assist as required.

iv. Feedback: Collect a few words off of each group and put onto the board. From here there are several possibilities: primary/secondary word stress, word families, opposites, hyponyms etc.… What you decide to do at this point will depend on the needs of your students.

Listening: The Teacher's Scar

i.   Tell students that you are going to tell them the story of how you got a particular scar. Have them listen to you tell the story and make notes.

ii. Students then check their versions of your story with a partner.

iii. Put the students into teams of four. The task is to make questions about your story to ask the other teams. Go round and help them with question formation but be careful not to give away correct answers as this will cause problems in the next stage.

iv. When teams have come up with about four or five questions, they ask each other. You can award points for correct answers. The team which gets the most answers right is the winner.

Speaking: The Students' Turn

i.   Put students in groups of four. Each person tells their own scar story. The group then chooses the most interesting story from the four.

ii. The group of four joins up with another group (which creates a new group of eight). The two most popular stories are then retold and the "best" one is chosen.

iii. When the class has chosen its favorite scar story, you can do the subsequent follow-up activity.

Rotation Writing: Retelling The Story

i. Put students in pairs and give each pair a piece of paper. Nominate one student as the pair's secretary but impress upon them that both students have to agree on what goes down on paper. Their task is to write the last scar story. Give them a few minutes to get going. When they have been writing for five minutes or so, stop them. (This will invariably lead to cries of "but we haven't finished yet!"). Then rotate the papers round one pair. The beauty of this exercise is that it incorporates all four macro-skills. Students have to read what has been written by a previous pair, talk about what to write next with their own partner, listen to what their partner suggests and then write it down. Rotate the papers as often as you feel like, but probably once every four minutes or so will be sufficient.

ii. When the stories are all completed, allocate one version to each pair and have them search for errors. If you prefer you could use the rotate technique again, perhaps nominating each pair to look for particular kinds of error, (spelling, punctuation, tenses, grammar and so on).

23. Travel Situations

Aims
i.   To give practice in speaking in the context of various travel situations.
ii. To give speaking and writing practice in a variety of functions (e.g.: permission, requests, *Wh*-questions).
iii. To give practice in asking for clarification.

Getting Ready
Some pieces of paper which should be torn up into strips. Each group of students will require eight strips of paper.

Procedure

Warmer

i.   Brainstorm places where you need to speak English when you go on holiday

e.g. At a pub—buying a drink

At a restaurant—ordering a meal

At a hotel—checking in

ii. Game: In pairs, students come up with as many places and things done as possible within a given time limit (three minutes?).

iii. Feedback: The pair with the most places and things done is the winner.

Language Focus: Where Are We?

i.   Put the following on the board (while students are doing *Warmer*?).

Just a little off the sides please. Leave the top long.	_____
Go to the end of the road. It's opposite the florist.	_____
Ten liters of unleaded please.	_____
Two first class stamps to Japan please.	_____
This way please. I'll show you to your table.	_____
Two adults and a child for Screen Two please.	_____
Go past the elevators and the pool's on your left.	_____
I'd like to hire a mini-van for the weekend.	_____
Would you like to try it on, sir?	_____
I'm afraid we're out of stock in that size, madam.	_____

ii. In pairs, students come up with the following:

a) where the utterance would be made

b) who would say it

iii. Monitor/assist as required.

iv. Feedback: Go over answers.

Writing: The Things Tourists Say

i.   Elicit from the class a couple of questions that tourists might ask when they are overseas in various places.

ii. Divide students into groups of three or four.

iii.   Hand out the strips of paper to each group (see: *Getting Ready*).

iv.   In groups, students write one question a tourist might ask on each strip.

v.   Monitor/assist as required. Check spelling and use of correct function.

   IMPORTANT: Make sure that the students' writing is clear and easy to read.

Speaking: What Am I Saying?

i.   Collect the strips from the students and rotate them round one group. Place them face-down in front of the group so that the writing cannot be seen.

ii.   Each group should now have eight strips which they themselves did not write.

iii.   Game: Students then play a mime game. Student A takes a strip and reads it. S/he has to communicate the question that is written there but is **not allowed to speak** at all. The other students in the group have to try and guess what is written on the strip exactly, based on the student's mime.

iv.   When they guess correctly, another student takes a new strip and the process is repeated.

v.   The first group to guess all eight correctly is the winner.

vi.   You may want to get one or two of the more dramatic students to perform for the class at the end of the lesson as a warm-down.

NB: You might like to do one yourself for the class at the beginning to make sure the students get the idea.

24. Where Are My Car Keys?

Aims
i.   To sensitize students to the role of contrastive stress in conversation.
ii. To give students practice in contrastive stress.
iii. To give students practice in speaking in the context of creating a dialogue.

Getting Ready
This lesson requires no special preparation.

Procedure

Language Focus: Working Out Meaning

i.   Write the following sentence on the board:

> I left my keys on the coffee table

ii.   Drill students chorally and/or individually six times. Each time, have them place primary stress on a different word. So you get something like:

> **I** left my keys on the coffee table (1st time)
> I **left** my keys on the coffee table (2nd time)
> I left **my** keys on the coffee table (3rd time) etc. …
> **NB**: No stress on "the"

iii. Discussion: Ask students if they think the different stress effects communicative value. You could, if you prefer, ask the question and have students discuss it in pairs or small groups.

iv.   Write the following (possible) meanings for the utterances on the board:

> a. not my brother's keys
> b. not under it
> c. do I have my keys now?
> d. it wasn't my wife who left them there
> e. not my wallet
> f. not the television

v.   In pairs, students match the meaning with the appropriate stress pattern.
vi.   Feedback: Check students answers, then lead into the first practice activity.

Listening: Communicative Meaning

i.   Say the sentence using one of the stress patterns.
ii.   Students have to guess which meaning you are conveying. Do this a couple of times.
iii. Students continue in pairs. Monitor and model/correct where necessary.

Reading And Speaking I: Experimenting With Meaning

i.   Write the following dialogue on the board:

      (John and Paul are on their way to a party)

    Paul: Oh darn!

    John: What's the matter, Paul?

    Paul: I left my keys on the coffee table.

    John: Don't worry, I'll get them. On the television did you say?

    Paul: No, the coffee table.

    John: That's right, under the coffee table.

    Paul: No, the keys are on the coffee table.

    John: Okay. (goes inside). Sorry, Paul. Was that your wallet?

    Paul: No, my keys John.

    John: I've got my keys Paul.

    Paul: Not your keys, John. My keys.

    John: Yeah, sorry Paul.

ii.   In pairs, students read the dialogue and decide on where to place primary stress.

iii. Monitor students, and then have them practice in pairs.

iv.   Get one or two of the better pairs to act out the conversation in front of the class.

Speaking II: The Students' Turn

i.   Put students in pairs.

ii.   Put a list of situations on the board:

    Checking in at a hotel; Asking for information at the airport;

    A family conversation over breakfast

iii. Students prepare a dialogue for one of the situations incorporating examples of contrastive stress.

iv.   Monitor/assist as required.

v.   Feedback: Students perform conversations for other pairs/whole class.

25. The Future I

Aims

i.   To give practice in use of future forms.
ii. To give practice in all four skills in the context of talking about the world's future.
iii. To develop vocabulary related to the fields of business, politics, entertainment, education.

Getting Ready

Students will need one piece of paper per pair. You will also need some adhesive tape if you choose to do *Writing and Speaking III, vii.*

Procedure

Warmer

i.   Put the following on the board:

MY GREAT-GRANDPARENTS' TIME; MY GRANDPARENTS' TIME; MY PARENTS' TIME

ii. In pairs, students list as many changes in society/the world that these people witnessed.

iii. You may need to give one or two examples (e.g. sexual equality: parents', space travel: parents', mass production: great-grandparents').

iv. Stress to students that the changes can have to do with any aspect of life, from the most trivial to the most dramatic.

v.   Monitor/assist as required.

vi. Feedback: Get some of the students to volunteer their answers.

Vocabulary And Speaking I: Present Trends

i.   Put the following categories on the board:

EDUCATION; WORK; FAMILY LIFE; GOVERNMENT; ENTERTAINMENT

ii. Ask students to think of things that are currently changing in these fields. Elicit one or two examples. If students are having trouble, give an example or two (e.g. more women are working full-time, the Internet etc. ...)

iii. In pairs/small groups, students come up with two things for each category.

iv. Monitor/assist as required.

v.   Change pairs/join pairs up to make groups of four. Students compare their ideas.

vi. Feedback: Get one or two students to tell the rest of the class their ideas.

Listening: The Teacher's Predictions

i.   Have students copy the four topics above on a new page.

ii. Tell students that you're going to tell them some of your predictions for the future. They have to listen and make notes under the relevant topic.

iii. Tell students some predictions.

iv. Students check in pairs.

v.   Tell students again.

vi.   Feedback: Put answers on board in note form for students to check against.

NB: You can think up your own ideas about the future or you can use the ones provided below.

Model Listening

1.   Children will no longer go to school. All teaching will be done via television.
2.   Holidays on Mars will become the latest fashion.
3.   Central government as we know it today will disappear. There will be no national level of government, just local councils or states.
4.   Women will no longer give birth naturally. All babies will be produced in infant laboratories.
5.   Every home in the world will have unlimited, clean, running water.
6.   Every home in the world will have a computer linking them to the Internet.
7.   Almost nobody will travel to an office in order to work. We'll all work from home.
8.   Films will become interactive. You will be able to change the story and decide the characters' fates be pressing buttons on your remote control.
9.   The United Nations will evolve into a World Government. All national governments will be gone.
10. Paper money and coins will be completely replaced by plastic cards.
11. Chinese will become a compulsory second language in all schools.
12. China will dominate the world's economy.

Speaking II: Will It Happen? When Will It happen?

i.   Put the following categories on the board:

> My Lifetime; My Children's Lifetimes;
> My Grand-children's Lifetimes

ii.   Put students into pairs or small groups.

iii. Students look back at your predictions and decide when they think they will happen. Students assign each prediction to either their own lifetime or those of their children or grandchildren.

iv.   Monitor/assist as required.

v.   Students change partners and compare ideas.

vi.   Students must then come up with a new compromise list after further discussion.

vii. Students then decide if the change is for the better or for the worse.

viii. Feedback: Have one or two groups offer their suggestions to the class.

ix.   Finally, you could give your own ideas to the class.

NB: Students can choose to say that the prediction will never come true if they like.

Writing And Speaking III: The Students' Thoughts

i.   Put students in pairs.

ii.   Have them choose one area from the first list (entertainment; government).

iii. Hand out one sheet of paper per pair. In pairs, students write a paragraph explaining their thoughts on how things will change in that area.

iv.   Monitor/assist as required. Let students use dictionaries if they need to.

v.   Collect in papers and redistribute.

26. Customs And Culture

∙∙

Aims
i.   To give practice in modal verbs (should(n't); have to/don't have to; mustn't; can/can't).
ii. To develop vocabulary for describing customs and cultures.
iii. To give students practice in speaking in the context of giving advice and information about their countries.

Getting Ready
This lesson requires no preparation.

Procedure

Warmer

i.   Write on board:

VERY SIMILAR TO MY OWN; QUITE SIMILAR TO MY OWN; TOTALLY DIFFERENT FROM MY OWN

ii.   Put students into small groups or pairs.

iii. Have students come up with two countries for each category.

iv.   Students change partners and discuss reasons for allocations.

NB: Try and get students to focus on cultural similarities rather than things like wealth, infrastructure or weather. For this reason it's probably a good idea for you to do your own country first. You could even have students ask you questions as to why you think so.

Vocabulary And Speaking I: India

i.   Ask students if they've ever been to India. If any say "yes," have them tell the class about it. Have other students ask questions. If "no," ask: "Would you like to go?" "Why?" or "Why not?"

ii.   Put the following categories on the board:

RELIGION; WEATHER; CLOTHES; FOOD; FAMOUS PLACES; SOUVENIRS

iii. In pairs, students come up with items for these categories.

iv.   Monitor/assist as required.

v.   Feedback: Get some of the students to come up to the board and write their ideas.

vi.   Check spelling as a class. **IMPORTANT**: Tell students either how many spelling mistakes there are or (for weaker groups) which words are spelled incorrectly.

Reading And Speaking II: Facts About India, True Or False?

i.   Write the following on the board:

You have to get a visa before you enter the country.

You mustn't eat with your left hand.

You can't go to certain parts of the country such as Kashmir.

You shouldn't pay the first price when you go shopping in a market.

You shouldn't pay the first price when you check into a five-star hotel.

You don't have to speak Hindi.

You can buy carpets and gems quite cheaply.

Women have to walk behind their husbands in public.

You should visit the Taj Mahal if you have time.

ii.   In pairs, students decide which of the above are true and which are false.

iii. Monitor/assist as required.

(Answers: T; F (right); T; T; F (hotels have fixed prices); T; T; F (not anymore!); T)

iv.   Feedback: Have class give their answers. Tell students correct answers.

v.   In pairs, students then rewrite false statements to make true ones.

NB: If you don't know anything about India, you can change the lesson to feature a country that you are more comfortable with.

Language Focus: The Meanings Of Modals

i.   Next to the quiz items, write the following on the board:

This is not possible, like it or not.

This is possible, like it or not.

In my opinion, I very strongly recommend that you don't do this.

I think this is a good idea, but it's your choice.

I think this is a bad idea, but it's your choice.

It is not necessary to do this.

This is required by law or is a rule.

ii.   Students look back at quiz and match one item to each of the above meanings.

iii. Monitor/assist as required.

iv.   Feedback: Give students correct answers. Explain any problems that **will** arise.

NB: You will probably need to explain the following points:

1.   *can* and *can't* do not really in themselves indicate the likelihood of something occurring merely the possibility or not.

2.   *should* and *shouldn't* aren't nearly as strong as students often think they are.

3.   *have to* and *don't have to* can best be explained as an external obligation. The authority exists outside of the speaker (e.g. The Indian authorities made the rules about visas, not me, I'm just telling you about the law).

4.   *must(n't)* expresses authority that rests with the speaker directly (e.g. eating with your right hand will cause great offense. I know this to be true and I am therefore telling you in the strongest possible terms).

Writing And Speaking III: Coming To My Country?

i.   Put students into pairs.

ii.   Put categories on the board:

IN THE HOME; EATING OUT; MEETING PEOPLE

iii.   Tell them that an old school friend is coming to (the country you are teaching in) and has written asking for advice about the place.

iv.   The person was a real bully at school so you want him/her to have a really bad time.

v.   In pairs, students come up with some bad advice for the school bully.

vi.   Monitor/assist as required.

vii.   Feedback: Get groups to read out their advice. Class chooses the best bad advice.

27. Weather

Aims
i.   To teach/review words for describing the weather.
ii. To give students practice in speaking in the context of talking about their weather preferences and deciding what people should do given particular aims in certain kinds of weather.
iii. To raise students' awareness of collocation.
iv. To give practice in the use of qualifiers: very; a bit; rather; quite.

Getting Ready
This lesson requires no special preparation.

Procedure

Warmer (no pun intended)

Class discussion:

i.   Put the following questions on the board:

> What kind of weather do you like best? What kind do you dislike?
>
> What's the worst weather you've ever experienced?
>
> How is today's weather different from yesterday's?
>
> Does the weather affect your mood?

ii. Students, in pairs/small groups discuss the above.
iii. Monitor/assist as required. Join in if you like.
iv. Feedback: Have one or two groups tell the class their opinions about the above.
     NB: Don't let it drag on though!

Vocabulary I: The Weather And The Seasons

i.   Put students in pairs.
     NB: For multinational classes, try to put students in a pair from their own country or if that's not possible, a neighboring country.
ii. Put on the board

> SPRING; SUMMER; AUTUMN; WINTER

iii. Students have to come up with different kinds of weather, both good and bad, for each of the seasons.
iv. Elicit one or two examples first.
v.   Monitor/assist as required. Let students use dictionaries if they want to.
vi. Students then change partners and compare ideas.
vii. Feedback: Have one or two students put some words on the board. Go over any spelling problems and do some pronunciation work.

Vocabulary II: Collocation: Adjectives And Nouns

i.   Put the following on the board:

A _____ wind	_____ rain	A _____ breeze
A _____ day	_____ snow	_____ fog
A _____ sky		

ii.   In pairs, students come up with two words for each space (so 14 words altogether).

iii.   Get students to use their dictionaries and point out that most good dictionaries will usually give the most common adjectives found with particular nouns.

iv.   Monitor/assist as required.

v.   Feedback: Get some students to come up to the board and give their answers.

Language Focus: Using Qualifiers

i.   Put the following countries on the board:

EGYPT; CANADA; FRANCE; JAPAN

ii.   Elicit what the weather is generally like in these countries. Allow room for debate but basically the class should be agreed on the following:

Egypt/hot; Canada/cold; France/temperate; Japan/cool (in autumn)

iii.   Then write the following on the board:

It's very cold here.

It's rather cold here.

It's quite cold here.

It's a bit cold here.

iv.   Tell students that an Egyptian, a Japanese, a Frenchman, and a Canadian went to London for a holiday in the spring. Ask students: Which tourist made which comment about the weather? Tell them that the temperature was 9° C (or 48° F).

v.   Students in pairs decide who said what.

vi.   Monitor/assist as required.

vii.   Feedback: Elicit answers: (They are: very/Egypt; rather/France; quite/Japan; a bit/Canada). Try to get across to students the notion of subjectivity in language choice. One's own experience informs the choice of qualifier. The four tourists all experience the same weather on that day, but will comment on it differently because they each have different norms to judge by.

Speaking I: What Would They Say Here?

i.   Put students in pairs and have them refer back to their country's typical weather for the four seasons (see: *Vocabulary I*).

ii.   Ask students to imagine what the four tourists would say about the weather in their country for the four seasons.

iii.   Students discuss their ideas in pairs/small groups.

iv.   Monitor/assist as required. Join in if you like.

v.   Feedback: Have one or two groups tell the class what they decided.

Speaking II: Where Should They Go?

i. Put the following on the board:

> Tom wants to open a scuba-diving shop.
>
> Sally wants to go hiking.
>
> Mr. and Mrs. Emly want to do a little sightseeing and visit the countryside.
>
> James would like to go skiing.
>
> Karen and Philip want to take a winter break.
>
> The Hodson family would like to spend a few days at a beach where
>
> it's not too hot, if possible.

ii. In pairs, students think about the weather in different parts of their country and at different times of the year. Students have to recommend somewhere for the above people to go.

iii. Students then join up to make groups of four.

iv. In each of their new groups, students compare ideas and come up with a new compromise list.

v. Monitor/assist as required. Join in if you like.

vi. Feedback: Get one or two groups to tell the class their recommendations.

28. Can You Give Me Some Advice?

Aims
i.   To give practice in all four skills in the context of asking for and giving advice.
ii. To review modal verbs (should, have to, ought to etc …).

Getting Ready
Each pair of students will need two pieces of paper. If you intend to do *Speaking and Writing II: Gentle Reader Variations One or Two*, you will need some adhesive tape or blue tack.

Procedure

Warmer

i.   Ask students: what kinds of problems do people usually ask advice for?

ii. Elicit one or two examples.

iii. If students just can't get it, write on the board:

> What shall I have for lunch today?
>
> Where shall I go on holiday this summer?
>
> I think my daughter is taking drugs. What should I do?
>
> Where can I get a good second-hand car?

Ask students: Which of these are easy to decide alone? Which would benefit from another person's input?

iv. Put the following on the board:

> Mother; Father; Brother; A close friend; An agony aunt (Brit.) / Advice Columnist (Am.)

In pairs, students come up with two examples of problems they would ask each person advice for (so ten problems altogether per pair).

v.   Feedback: Get one or two pairs to tell the class their ideas.

Listening: The Teacher's Problem

i.   Tell the students that you have a problem and you would like their advice.

ii. Tell students your problem. Students listen and make notes. Grade your language according to your class, but try and retain the features of natural speech (weak forms, liaison etc.).

iii. Students compare notes in pairs.

iv. Tell students again. Students improve their notes and check with their partner again.

NB: You can make up your own problem or use/adapt the one below.

Model Listening

I've got a bit of a problem and I'd really appreciate your advice, if you don't mind. At the bottom of my garden, I've recently started growing strawberries. It's a new hobby and I really enjoy it. I'm looking forward to picking and eating them. The thing is that my next-door-neighbor has a cat. Every night, it comes into my garden and chooses to go to the toilet in my strawberry bed. I know it's my neighbor's cat because I've caught him in the act a few times. Every time I see it, I chase it off but it always comes back. I can't stand guard twenty four hours a day—I have to go to work! I tried talking to my neighbor but he doesn't seem to care. In fact, I think he thinks it's a rather funny joke. What do you think I should do? Shall I put down some poisoned meat or just hit the bloody animal over the head with a shovel? No, just kidding! But short of killing the animal, which I don't want to do, I can't think of anything. Can you think of something?

Speaking I: What Should S/he Do?

i.   In pairs, students consider your problem and come up with advice for you.

ii. Pairs then join up to make groups of four and tell each other their recommendations. Each group should choose one course of action.

iii. Feedback: Get groups to give you their advice. You choose the one you like best.

Speaking II And Writing I: Advice Columns

i.   Ask students if they've ever read the advice page in a newspaper (either in English or their own language).

ii. Elicit the different sorts of problems people write in with.

iii. Ask: Do you like reading these kinds of letters? Why (not)?

iv. Put students in pairs. Hand out one piece of paper to each pair (see: *Getting Ready*).

v.   In pairs, students think of a problem and compose a letter to a newspaper advice column.
     NB: Stress that the student actually doing the writing is only the secretary. Both students have to agree on what goes down on paper.
     NB: You probably ought to set a time limit to encourage students to finish.

vi. Monitor/assist as required.
     NB: Give students a few prompt questions as you monitor and read their work in order to encourage interesting letters (e.g. I met a great new girl who I really like. Teacher Prompt: "Where did you meet?" "Why is she so great?" etc. ...).

vii. When students have finished, collect in the letters.

Speaking III And Reading I: What Should S/he Do?

i.   Hand out the letters so that each pair has a new letter.

ii. In pairs, students read and discuss the person's problem and a suitable course of action.

iii. Monitor/assist as required. Help with any problem vocabulary/structure.

Speaking IV And Writing II: Gentle Reader

i.   Hand out the second piece of paper (see: *Getting Ready*).

ii.   This time, the students are agony aunts. They have to compose a reply to the letter they received.

iii. Encourage students to be gentle with each other. Even if they think the problem is stupid or whatever, they don't want to be cruel to the writer.

iv.   Monitor/assist as required. Check use of target language (see: *Aims ii*).

v.   As before, students have to cooperate and agree on what goes into the reply. The student with the pen does not have more authority than the one who does not.

vi.   The reply is then given to the pair who composed it.

vii. Students read the advice and then pair up and discuss the advice, whether they think it's good or not, why it wouldn't work and so on.

Variation One

i.   Collect in the advice and redistribute so that everyone reads advice to a problem they themselves did not compose.

ii.   In pairs, students have to imagine what the original letter was.

iii. Stick the original problem letters around the classroom. Students read and try and find the letter that goes with the advice they have.

Variation Two

i.   Collect in the letters giving the advice.

ii.   Pin them around the classroom.

iii. Students wander around the room and have to locate the advice that corresponds to the problem that they wrote about in their original letter.

29. Wordbuilding II

· ·

Aims
i.   To teach/review relationships between word families.
ii. To give students practice in speaking in the context of asking and answering a
     questionnaire.

Getting Ready
Students will need a copy of the question sheet each.

Procedure

Warmer

i.   Write the following sayings on the board:

     Early to bed, early to rise, makes a man ____ , ____ and ____.

     Love of money is the root of all ____.

     ____ is in the eye of the beholder.

     A ____ and his money are soon parted.

ii. In pairs, students try to come up with suitable words to complete the sayings.

iii. Monitor/assist as required. Allow students to be as creative as they like. They don't
     have to come up with the correct word.

iv. Feedback: Get some of the students to offer suggestions.

v.   Tell students the original words (Answers: healthy, wealthy, wise, evil, beauty, fool).

Speaking I: What Do You Think?

i.   Put following questions on the board:

     Do you agree with the sayings or not? Why?;

     Why and how do you think the sayings began?;

     Are there sayings like this in your own language?;

     Can you translate any into English?

ii. In pairs /small groups, students discuss the questions.

iii. Monitor/assist as required. Join in if you like.

iv. Feedback: Get one or two groups to tell the class their ideas.

Reading and Vocabulary: A Questionnaire

i.   Hand out copies of the worksheet to each student (see: *Getting Ready*).

ii. In pairs, students read and check the meaning of any unknown words.

iii. Monitor/assist as required. Let students use their dictionaries.

Speaking II: Conducting A Survey

i.   Put students in pairs. Each pair has to choose six questions from the list which
     they'd like to ask other members of the class.

ii. When students have chosen their six, have them divide them evenly so that each student is responsible for asking three questions.

iii. Students then mingle and ask their questions to as many other students as possible, making a note of the answers.

iv. Monitor/assist as required. Join in if you like.

v. Students then go back into their pairs and report what they found out.

vi. Feedback: Get students to tell the class the most common answers to the questions. **NB**: Don't take up too much time with the feedback though.

Language Focus: Word Families

i. Write on the board:

BEAUTY

ii. Then write the following sentences:

_____ is in the eye of the beholder.

It's a _____ day today.

She dances _____.

They _____ the room with a new coat of paint.

iii. In pairs, students complete the sentences with a form of the word *beauty*.

iv Ask students to give the grammatical name for the different forms. Teach: noun; adjective; verb; adverb.

v. Students then look back at the question sheet and choose four words from the six questions they asked in *Speaking I*.

vi. In pairs, students come up with the word families for those four words.

vii. Monitor/assist as required. Let students use their dictionaries.

Writing And Speaking III: The Students' Questions

i. In pairs, tell students to write their own questions using a different form of the word from the six questions.

ii. Monitor/assist as required.

iii. In small groups this time, students ask their questions and discuss.

iv. Monitor/assist as required. Join in if you like.

What's Your Opinion?

Which is more important: wealth or happiness?

Which is more important when buying a car: reliability or comfort?

What achievement in your life are you most proud of?

Have you ever been seriously ill?

Who is the most interesting person you know?

Do you ever think about security in your old age?

Who would you rather marry: someone that's old and rich or young and poor?

Have you got a secret ambition?

Who do you admire most in History?

Do you believe in Life after Death?

Do you think being famous is a blessing or a curse?

Should a democratic society allow private education?

30. What Do You Think?

....

Aims

i. To give practice in speaking in the context of asking for and giving opinions, agreeing and disagreeing.

ii. To teach/review functions for expressing the above.

Getting Ready

i. Copy the six topics given in *Warmer*. Make one copy per group, cut them up so there is one topic per strip of paper.

ii. Each group will require one board game each. If you have access to dice, bring these along too.

Procedure

Warmer

Play game: *Hidden Topics*.

i. Copy the topics below onto a separate bit of paper.

ii. Divide class into groups of 4—6 players.

iii. Put the strips in a pile face down in front of them (see: *Getting Ready*).

iv. One student takes a topic from the pile and shows it only to the person on their right.

v. The two of them start talking about the topic indirectly. They mustn't refer to the topic outright.

vi. The other students listen and when they think they know what the topic is, they can join in the conversation.

vii. If, in the course of the conversation it transpires that the latest member has got the wrong end of the stick, they are awarded a point and have to drop out.

viii. The last person able to join in the conversation is also awarded a point.

ix. When the topic is exhausted, a new player takes a new topic and the game starts again.

x. The player with the most points at the end of the game is the loser.

Possible Topics For The Game

Going to the hairdressers'	Taxi Drivers	Staying in on Saturday night
Places to go on a first date	Fast Food	Missing your last train home

Language Focus: Opinions

i. Write the following dialogues on the board:

_____ hip-hop music?

_____ it's awful.

_____ . It's the worst music I've ever heard.

I really like living in the country.

_____ . It's too quiet and boring.

I don't like the new James Bond movie very much.

_____ . The action's great and the Bond Girls are really cute.

I don't enjoy Christmas very much anymore.

_____ . It's too much hassle and too expensive.

ii.   In a separate box on the board, write:

So do I; Neither do I; What do you think of…?; I think; I do ; I don't

iii.   In pairs, students put the functions into the spaces.
iv.   Monitor/assist as required.
v.   Feedback: Get two or three students to come up to the board and write their answers.
vi.   Concept Check: Ask students: In which of the conversations do the speakers have the same opinion? In which do they have different opinions?

Pronunciation: Stress And Intonation

i.   Drill the students as a group (choral).
ii.   Point out the stress in the short answers, **I** do and **I** don't. Students almost always have difficulty with this.
iii.   Teach the intonation pattern: ^{so} do ^{I} Ne $_{ither}$ $_{do}$ $_{I}$
iv.   In pairs, students then practice dialogues.
v.   Monitor/model as required.

Vocabulary And Speaking I: Do We Agree Or Not?

i.   Put the following topics on the board:

Kinds of fruit; music; films; sports; actors; musicians/pop groups.

ii.   Each student (on their own) write three things or people that they like and three they dislike (e.g. jazz ✓ bananas ✓ tennis ✓ David Bowie ✗ Demi Moore ✗ Horror ✗)
iii.   Melee: Students then walk around and tell each other the things they like and dislike.
       Task: Students try to find six different people who either agree or disagree with them.
iv.   Monitor/assist as required. Check use of target language (see: *Aims*).

Speaking II: Board Game: What Do You Think?

i.   Divide class into groups of four to six players.
ii.   Give each group a copy of the board game on the next page.
       NB: It's probably a good idea to enlarge the photocopy.
iii.   Each student takes out a coin or other small object which serves as their counter.
iv.   Students take turns to flip a coin. Heads, students go forward one square, Tails, they go forward two squares.
v.   Students land on a particular topic and give their opinion about it. Other students listen and agree and disagree. Hopefully this will on occasion, turn into an interesting discussion.
vi.   When the topic is exhausted, the next student flips a coin.
vii.   Monitor/assist as required. Join in if you like.

What Do You Think?

START

Americans

High school students

Classical music

Men with long hair

New York

Eating meat

Where you live

Bunjee Jumping

Mobile phones

Smoking

Scuba diving

University life

Taxi drivers

FINISH

A holiday in Europe

Princess Diana

Chinese food

Riding the subway

Window shopping

Perfume

Today's weather

31. Tricky Situations

....

Aims
i.   To review/teach various functions for permission, requests, apologizing and inviting.
ii. To give speaking practice in the context of roleplays related to *i*.

Getting Ready
Each student will need a copy of the language work worksheet. Students will also need copies of the rolecards.

Procedure

Warmer

i.   Divide class into two groups, A and B.

ii.   Divide the two groups into pairs (so 20 students = five A pairs and five B pairs).

iii. Give each pair one role card, either A1 or B1.

iv.   Students read their role card and decide with their partner how to tackle the situation.

v.   Tell them they can make notes if they want to, but you're going to take the role cards away from them.

vi.   Pair Students A and Students B. (so 20 students = 10 pairs).

vii. Students roleplay situation.

    NB: Make sure students realize that the situations are simultaneous not consecutive. The roleplay situations (as you will see) have some element of conflict built into them.

viii. Students return to their first partner, discuss what happened in their situation and what the outcome was.

Language Focus I: Functions

i.   Put the following categories on the board:

        PERMISSION; REQUESTING; INVITING; APOLOGIZING; POSSIBLE RESPONSES

ii.   In pairs, students come up with different expressions to perform the functions. Elicit one or two examples first from the class.

iii. Monitor/assist as required.

iv.   Feedback: Have students put up some possibilities (three per category?) on the board.

v.   Then add steps to each box. In pairs, students put the various functions from most formal (top) to least formal (at the bottom).

vi.   Feedback: Go over students' work. Correct as necessary.

vii. Concept Check: Ask students what factors influence the level of politeness used?
    Elicit: Relationship, What you want, Urgency, Place. Then put on board:

	a friend	to open the door
	your boss	to close the window
Ask	your father	for a $10,000 loan
	your boss	for a pay rise
	a friend	if you can use his mobile phone
	a friend	if you can use his car

In pairs, students to decide which function would be most appropriate in each situation.

Language Focus II: Make It Appropriate

i.   Hand out one copy of the Language Work sheet to each student.

ii.   In pairs, students read and rewrite the items so that they sound more appropriate.

iii. Monitor/assist as required.

Speaking: A Tricky Situation

The procedure for this activity is exactly the same as for the first roleplay (see: *Warmer*). Just substitute role cards A2 and B2. Try and have students work with different people this time.

TRICKY SITUATIONS: LANGUAGE WORK

Work with another student. Rewrite the following sentences so that they are more appropriate.

1. Waiter (to customer): Hurry up and finish. We want to go home now.

2. Man (to friend): Sorry to trouble you, but do you think I could possibly use your toilet?

3. Man (to stranger): What time is it now?

4. Man in Burning House (to stranger): Hello there. I was just wondering if you wouldn't mind calling the fire brigade. You see, it is rather hot in here.

5. Hotel Clerk (to guest): Fill in the form and try not to steal the pen.

6. Student (to teacher): I don't feel too good so I'm going home. Okay?

7. Boss (to secretary): Would you mind awfully typing this letter, if you're not too busy that is?

8. Boy (to girl he likes): I'm going to the cinema on Friday. You coming or not?

9. Ticket Inspector (to passenger): Show me your ticket now.

10. Man (to stranger): Give me your paper. You're not reading it and I want to.

ROLE CARDS FOR TRICKY SITUATIONS

●ROLE CARD A1

You are a university student. You have just moved to your new college and have rented a small apartment. As the university is far from your hometown, you do not know anybody in the area. You haven't made many new friends yet so most evenings you just sit at home and listen to the radio or watch TV. You're feeling a bit bored with your life and you want to start meeting some new people. Go to your next-door neighbor. Introduce yourself and invite him/her out for a pizza and a drink this evening.

●ROLE CARD B1

You are a fourth-year university student. You are trying to study very hard for your end-of-year exams. Your grades have not been very good over the last year so you want to make sure you get a good score on the test. Every night you come home straight from college to study and review what you learned in class that day. Recently however, a new person has moved into the apartment next door. The person stays up until quite late at night playing the radio or the television and the noise is disturbing you. You are finding it difficult to concentrate on your work. Go to your neighbor. Explain your situation. Ask him to make less noise.

●ROLE CARD A2

This coming Saturday is your tenth wedding anniversary. To celebrate, you and your husband/wife are going out for a very special dinner. You have made a reservation for 7:00 p.m. at the restaurant where you went on your first date. Unfortunately there is a problem: your baby daughter, Naomi. She is only four years old and needs a babysitter. The girl who promised to sit for you phoned up yesterday to tell you that she has caught a really bad cold and cannot babysit for you on Saturday. You don't want to cancel the dinner. Go to your friend. Explain the situation. Ask him if he can babysit for you on Saturday instead.

●ROLE CARD B2

A month ago, you met a new boy/girl. Your relationship is going really well and it is time to meet his/her parents. For this important first meeting, you have arranged to go out for a drive in the country and have a picnic by the sea. You have been planning it for a couple of weeks and everyone is really looking forward to the day, which is this Saturday. Unfortunately this morning, someone reversed into the back of you and although you are not hurt, your car has been damaged. It will take ten days to repair it. You do not want to cancel the day out. Go to your friend. Explain the situation. Ask him/her to lend you their car for the day.

✂

32. Advertising

Aims
i.   To give students practice in speaking and listening in the context of discussing attitudes to advertising, preparing a commercial and describing commercials.
ii. To develop vocabulary related to the field of advertising.
iii. To give students practice in expressing and asking for opinions.

Getting Ready
This lesson requires no special preparation unless you plan to do *Warmer, Variation.*

Procedure

Warmer

i.   Put up some slogans on the board: e.g.

Speak _____   It's a _____   00 _____

_____ lager   4400111 _____

Come to where the _____ is, _____ country

(Answers: Lark, Sony, wonderful, Do, Weekly mansion, flavor, Marlboro)

NB: The above slogans are common in Japan. You will need to change some or all of them according to the country in which you are teaching.

ii. In pairs, students try and fill in the blanks to complete the slogan.
iii. Feedback: Have one or two students come up to the board and write their answers. Check students' efforts.

Variation

i.   Cut out some advertisements from magazines. You will need about four per group.
ii. Put students in groups of about four. Distribute ads.
iii. Ask students: Have they seen any of them before? If yes, can they remember in which magazine they saw them in? Do they like the ad.? Why (not)? Do they think it's effective? To whom is it trying to appeal?
iv. Then get students to decide how the advertiser is trying to get them to buy the product (e.g. using comedy, sex, an expert, the exotic and so on).
v.   Students divide ads into relevant categories.

NB: This would also work if incorporated into *Speaking II: Images in Advertising.*

Vocabulary: Words Connected With Advertising

i.   Write the word: ADVERTISING on the board in capitals.

ii.   Elicit from class a few words connected with this topic.

iii.   Then write these sub-categories on the board:

PLACES TO ADVERTISE; METHODS OF ADVERTISING; PEOPLE

Give an example for each sub-category (e.g. magazines, hard-sell, consumer).

iv.   In pairs/small groups, students continue adding to the sub-categories .

v.   Monitor/assist as required.

vi.   Feedback: Get one or two of the students to write their ideas on the board.

Listening I: Spot The Commercial

i.   Ask Students: Do you have a favorite TV commercial? Why do you like it? Is there a commercial you dislike? Why?
       NB: This can be done as a class discussion or in small groups.

ii.   Tell students you're going to describe a commercial. They have to listen and raise their hand as soon as they know the product being advertised.

iii.   Describe a commercial. Students listen and try and guess the product.

NB: Teachers in Japan may wish to use the advertisement described below. For those of you teaching elsewhere, use a local commercial.

Model Listening

It's early evening in a city in Japan, probably Tokyo. Three office workers have just left the office after a day's work. One of them suggests that they should all go for a drink after such a tough day. One of the other two is rather keen on the idea but the other apologizes, saying that he has a prior appointment. That's when the other two remember that tonight is their colleague's English class.

(Answer: Nova Language School)

Speaking I And Listening II: The Students' Turn

i.   Put students in pairs.

ii.   Student A describes a commercial to his/her partner.

iii.   Student B listens and tries to guess the product as fast as possible.

iv.   When Student B has guessed (or given up), the roles are reversed.

v.   Students note down how many seconds it took them to get each commercial.

vi.   Students should describe three commercials each (so six in total).

vii.   The student who takes the least time to guess all three commercials together is the winner.

Speaking II: Images In Advertising

i.   Ask students to list some techniques advertisers use to make their ads. memorable.

ii. Elicit themes such as sex, comedy, the voice of authority, a famous face.

iii. Put students into small groups. Students think of two advertisements for each category;
     two commercials that use comedy, two for sex, two for famous face etc. ...,
     one of which they feel succeeded in making the product desirable, one which did not.
     Students have to come up with reasons as to why they think so.

iv. Monitor/assist as required. Join in if you like.

v.   Feedback: Get one or two groups to tell the class about one commercial.

Speaking III: Sell The School

i.   Put students in groups. Tell them they have to prepare a 30-second commercial to
     advertise the school/university where they are studying English.

ii. Monitor/assist as required.

iii. Feedback: Get students to perform their advertisements for the class.

NB: This activity, if it takes off, can last a whole lesson in itself.

33. Job Search

....

Aims

i. To give speaking practice in the context of designing and doing a survey.
ii. To review modal verbs (should (be); has to (be); ought to (be);)
iii. To give practice in writing, especially question forms and notetaking.
iv. To review/build vocabulary for describing attributes and characteristics.

Getting Ready

This lesson does not require any special preparation.

Procedure

Warmer

i. Put a list of well-known people on the board. e.g.

> Sean Connery; Madonna; Eric Clapton; Bill Clinton

NB: These can be nationally or internationally famous people, or even people that only your students will know: other teachers, the principal for example.

ii. Tell students that these people are tired of the jobs they are doing now and would like to try something **completely** different.

iii. In pairs, students come up with alternative occupations for the people on the board. **NB**: Stress to students that their academic qualifications should not be taken into consideration. They ought to base their decision on the sort of person they are.

iv. In pairs or small groups, students discuss alternative jobs for the people.

v. Monitor/assist as required. Join in if you want.

vi. Feedback: Get one or two groups to tell their choices to the class.

Vocabulary: Characteristics And Attributes

i. Put the following jobs on the board:

> Doctor; Stunt man; Policeman; Hotel Receptionist

ii. Ask Students: What sort of people make good _____?

iii. Elicit one or two adjectives (friendly, intelligent, patient and so on…)

iv. In pairs, students come up with four adjectives for each job.
IMPORTANT: They can use each word only once. (so 16 words altogether).

v. Let students use dictionaries if they want to or ask you.
Check use of target language (see: *Aims ii and iv*).

vi. Students change partners and compare their work. Students then have to come up with a new list with their new partner. This will require them to justify the choices they have already made and reach some sort of compromise.

vii. Feedback: Get one or two pairs to tell the class what they decided.

Writing And Speaking I: Designing A Questionnaire

i. Ask students if they have ever filled in a Job Suitability Questionnaire. If any students have, ask them what kind of questions were on it and whether the job suggested for them was one they'd like to do. If they haven't, explain briefly what it is. (Basically, it asks questions which try to discover things about the person's character, strong and weak points in order to suggest a field they might think about going into).

ii. Tell students that they are going to design one and then interview each other to find suitable jobs for each other.

iii. Give students one or two examples of the kinds of questions that are often asked.

e.g. Do you get angry quickly?

Have you ever gone white-water rafting?

Do you like to work in a team?

iv. Elicit one or two more questions from the class.

v. Put students in pairs. Students to come up with at least ten more questions for their questionnaire.

vi. Monitor/assist as required.

NB: Make sure that both students write down the questions.

Note taking And Speaking II: Interview The Client

i. Get students to think of a job that they would realistically like to do either after graduating or instead of the job they're doing at the moment.

ii. Regroup the students so that they are with a new partner.

iii. Students interview each other and note down their new partner's answers.

iv. Students then go back to their first partner, (the one with whom they designed their questionnaire).

v. Students discuss the answers they got and try to think of a job that would be suitable for their "clients."

vi. When they have decided, students go back to the "client" and tell them what job (or sort of work) they recommend and why.

vii. Students then show the interviewer the job they had written down at the beginning of the exercise. Students then discuss they suitability (or not) of that occupation for the person.

34. Noun Phrases

Aims
i.   To give practice in position of adjectives in the noun phrase.
ii. To give practice in developing complex sentences.

Getting Ready
This lesson requires no special preparation.

Procedure

Warmer

i.   Write the following on the board:

a. a young beautiful girl	d. a romantic summer warm evening
b. a wooden Italian expensive table	e. a second-hand dangerous station wagon
c. a Chinese rare priceless vase	f. a tall French handsome dark man

ii. Put students in pairs or small groups.

iii. Have them rearrange the adjectives in each of the clauses so that they "sound" or "feel" right.

iv. Feedback: Check students' efforts.

Speaking I: Discussing Meaning

i.   Ask students if they know of any rules concerning word order in noun phrases. Some of them will probably have come across the theory that the order is: Value (beautiful, expensive), Size (big, small), Age (old, new), Shape (square, round) Color (blue, dyed) Origin (French, Tudor) Material (woolen, plastic) Compound, Headword.
While not misleading, it is rather a lot to expect a student to retain. There is perhaps a simpler way to remember the order which is as follows:

1. The more objective the sense of the word, the nearer it goes to the headword.
e.g. A beautiful young girl.
More people would agree that the girl is young (objective) than that she is beautiful (subjective).

2. The more permanent the sense of the word, the nearer it is to the headword.
e.g. A young French man
Clearly, with the passage of time, the man's youth will give way to middle and then, old age. He will, however, remain French until his death.

If the noun phrase contains a mixture of both kinds of adjective, then the temporary/permanent adjectives are located closer than the subjective/objective adjectives.
Stress to students that this rule is not written in stone but can serve as a useful guideline.

In order to teach Rules 1 and 2 above you could do the following:
i.   Go back to examples a—f which are now written on the board in the correct word order.
ii. Get students, in pairs, to divide the adjective into groups: Fact; Opinion; Fixed; Changing

iii. When they have done so, ask them if they can see a pattern emerging in the noun phrase.

iv. Go over the rule with the class, answering any questions which may come up.

IMPORTANT: Stress that there is room for debate. In fact the more they discuss, the more they'll get from it and the greater they will be sensitized to the nature of adjectival order.

Speaking II: Experimenting With Meaning

i. Write the following sentence on the board:

> In the classroom, there was a teacher.

ii. Tell students that you are going to give them some extra information. They have to insert the extra information in the original sentence.

iii. Write the following up on the board:

> The classroom was small.

Elicit: In the small classroom, there was a teacher.

iv. Continue with the following information.

NB: If you don't like my suggestions, feel free to come up with your own. It's the idea that's important.

> The teacher was tall.
> The classroom was dark.
> The teacher was tired.
> The classroom was frightening.
> The teacher was handsome.
> The classroom was hot.
> The teacher was American.
> The classroom was round.
> The teacher was teaching the past simple.
> The classroom was dirty.

As each new piece of information is added, drill the students, more for affective reasons than anything else.

IMPORTANT: Don't let students write anything down during this stage. It works much better if they try to rely on short-term memory at this point.

When it has been drilled for the last time, put students in pairs and have them write down the whole thing.

Speaking III: Creating Meaning

i. Put students in pairs.

ii. Have students come up with their own sentences.

iii. Monitor/assist as required.

iv. Then have pairs change partners or make groups of four. Students have to build up the noun phrases together. You could, if you wish, create some sort of points system awarded for the longest, funniest, most ridiculous sentence in the class!

35. Talking About Your Life

Aims
i.   To contrast past tense forms (especially simple, continuous and perfect).
ii. To give speaking practice in the context of talking about one's life.
iii. To give writing practice in the context of composing a biography.

Getting Ready
Each student will need one piece of paper.

Procedure

Warmer

i.   Write the following on the board:

> Where do you live?
>
> Do you like your home/area? Why?
>
> Have you ever lived anywhere else? When?
>
> Which place do you like the best/least? Why?

ii. Have students ask you the above questions. Encourage follow-up questions.

iii. In pairs, students ask and answer the above questions.

iv. Monitor/assist as required.

Speaking I And Note Taking I: Places I've Lived

i.   Get students to draw a time line for their life.

ii. On it, students mark the different places they've lived. e.g.

70	81	82	86	87	NOW
Leicester	Cardiff	London	Kathmandu	Hong Kong	Tokyo

iii. Students then interview two other students and draw their time lines underneath.

Language Focus: Contrasting Tenses

i.   Put your own time line onto the board.

ii. Draw a second time line on the board and elicit some information from the students about where they have lived. Put this onto the board: e.g.

70	81	87	90	97	NOW
Kenji	Kenji	Yoko	Yoko	Hiroshi	Hiroshi
Tokyo	Osaka	Sapporo	Tokyo	Meguro	Ikebukuro

iii. Put prompts on the board comparing places where students have lived with where you have lived. Elicit/teach the following structures:

> e.g. While I was living in Leicester, Kenji was living in Tokyo.
>
> I lived in Cardiff for four years.
>
> Yoko moved to Tokyo after I'd left Hong Kong.

iv.   Get students to explain the differences between the three structures.

Speaking II: Comparing Where We've Lived

i.   Put students into new pairs.

ii.   Students look at time lines and make statements about where they and other students have lived. This may seem a bit mechanical but it is a useful opportunity for them to experiment with the structures.

iii. Monitor/assist as required.

Speaking III and Note Taking II: Other Things We've Done

i.   Get students to draw four more time lines like the ones below:

Education   _____

Holidays   _____

Good Experience   _____

Bad Experience   _____

ii.   In pairs, students interview each other and make notes on the time line about their partner (schools they went to, places they've visited and so on…).

iii. Students then compare their lives (While you were living in Paris, I went to Spain on holiday etc. …).

iv.   Monitor/assist as required.

Writing: A Biography

i.   Hand out a blank piece of paper to each student.

ii.   Using the information gained from the previous exercise, students write a paragraph about their partner's life.
      IMPORTANT: They must not write the name of the person on the page, only some information.

iii. Collect in the papers and redistribute so that each student has neither their own biography nor the one they wrote.

iv.   Melee: Students mingle, ask each other questions and try to find the person to whom the biography belongs.

36. The Future II

∙∙∙

Aims
i.   To review/practice use of future forms (especially future perfect; future continuous).
ii. To review/practice modals to talk about the future (e.g. might; will ; probably; should).
iii. To review time expressions (by the time; before; as soon as possible; until etc …).
iv. To give practice in speaking in the context of talking about their own futures.

Getting Ready
This lesson requires no special preparation.

Procedure

Warmer

i.   Get students to list four things they expect to do this week; four things they expect to do within the next five years; four things they expect to do within the next twenty years; one thing they'd really like to do before they die.

NB: If you have somewhat elderly students, you might wish to drop this last option!

ii. Students in pairs then compare and discuss each others' hopes.

iii. Feedback: Have one or two students tell the class their hopes/plans.

Listening: The Teacher's Future

i.   Tell students that you're going to tell them about how you see your life going over the next few years. They have to listen and put the events into one of the following categories.

Write on the board:

CERTAIN   VERY LIKELY   SMALL CHANCE   A HOPE

ii. Students listen and take notes under the appropriate heading.

iii. Students check in pairs.

iv. Tell students again. Students check again.

v.   Feedback: Have one or two students come up to the board and write their answers.

NB: The model given below is one I have often used in class. It is there as a model for you although if you wish to use it as it stands, I won't tell anyone!

Model Listening

Well, I think my life's going to change in some ways and not in others. I'm going to stay here in Japan for the next few years at least but I don't think we'll be living in the same place. I'd like to buy an apartment or a house if I can afford it fairly soon. I expect I'll be a father within the next couple of years coz I'm getting on a bit. As far as work is concerned, I'll probably stay where I am for the moment but at some point I'd like to move to a university nearer the city center. I don't know, if I were offered a position outside of Tokyo, I might take it. It depends on my wife, I guess. I'll have finished my Ph.D. by the time I'm 37 and I expect I'll have written a few books by then too. Health wise, I want to lose some weight so I'll be joining a sports club this year and I might even take up something like tennis. I don't really have too many hobbies anymore so I think

I'd like to start studying another language, perhaps Chinese or Thai. When I retire I might return to Europe although I do think that's not a serious option. I'll probably divide my time between Japan, India and Europe if I can afford to. Anyway, whatever happens, I hope that I'll be able to look back on an interesting life.

Language Focus: Degrees Of Certainty

i.   Put the following on the board:

A	B
I might change jobs	I'll probably change jobs
I want to join a sports club	I hope to join a sports club
I'll be living in Spain	I'd like to live in Spain
I'll have finished my education	I've finished my education
By the time I'm 40	Until I'm 40
It's likely I'll be a father	I may be a father

ii. In pairs, students discuss the pairs of sentences and decide whether they have basically the same or a different meaning.

iii. Monitor/assist as required.

iv. Feedback: Elicit answers from class.

Speaking: The Students' Futures

i.   Put up some prompts on the board:

education; family; home; job; hobbies; foreign travel

ii. Ask students how they see their life going in the future and what changes there might be. Have them refer to the prompts and try to think of two things for each category, one in the near future and one in the distant future.

iii. Students, in pairs, then tell each other about their respective futures. Encourage students to ask questions.

iv. Students listen and take notes.

v.   Monitor/assist as required. Join in if you like.

vi. Students then change partners and tell their new partner about their old partner.

vii. Feedback: Get one or two of the students to tell the class the most interesting thing they learned about either the student they interviewed or the one they heard about.

Notes